Designer
Knitting

Designer
Knitting

Nina Shuttlewood and Janet Biggs

Arco Publishing, Inc.
New York

First published 1984

Library of Congress Cataloging in Publication Data
Shuttlewood, Nina.
    Designer knitting.

    Bibliography: p.
    Includes index.
    1. Knitting   I. Biggs, Janet.   II. Title.
TT820.S524 1985   746.9'2   84-21696
ISBN 0-668-06446-3

Printed in Great Britain

Contents

ACKNOWLEDGEMENTS 7

INTRODUCTION 9

1 **The Ross System** *11*

2 **Pure Wool** *13*

Patterns for:
Slash-necked sweater *14*
Wedding dress *17*
Waistcoat *21*
Stole *24*
Lace, yoked sweater *26*
Lace-panelled sweater *29*
Man's jacket *32*
Lace-patterned sweater *35*

3 **Wool Blend** *38*

Patterns for:
V-necked sweater *39*
V-necked cabled sweater *42*

4 **Plyed Yarns** *45*

Patterns for:
Lace and cabled patterned sweater *45*
Smocked cardigan *48*
Triangular shawl *51*
Frilled V-necked sweater *53*

5 **Plyed Silk** *56*

Patterns for:
Skirt
Jacket
Camisole

6 **Use of Commercial Dyed Yarns** *61*

Colour blending *61*
Commercial dyeing (yarns) *87*

Patterns for:
Diamond-patterned sweater *62*
Child's jumper *65*
Girl's jumper *68*
Waistcoat *72*
Stocking-stitch sweater *75*
Bomber jacket *78*
Drop-shoulder sweater *81*
Lace and moss stitch sweater *84*
Knitted coat *87*
Commercial dyeing (garments) *90*
Man's V-necked cardigan *90*

7 **Luxury Fibres** *94*

Patterns for:
Short-sleeved sweater *94*
Fair Isle and lace pattern *97*
Cashmere sweater *101*
Double-breasted jacket *104*

8 Fun Fibres *107*

Patterns for:
Round-yoked sweater *107*
Hat *110*

9 Creating a Portfolio *112*

10 Technical Information *113*

Tension *113*
Knitting needles (sizes) *113*
Gram to ounce conversion *113*
Metric to Imperial conversion *114*

ABBREVIATIONS *115*

LIST OF SUPPLIERS *116*

BIBLIOGRAPHY *118*

INDEX *119*

Acknowledgements

We should like to thank the following:

Mabel Ross for allowing us to use the 'Ross System';

Keith Yuill, Maldon, Essex, for the photography;

Diane Ryder, Julie Green, Sarah March, Martin Harris and Joe Embling for modelling the garments;

All our hard-working knitters and a special thank you to Peter and Diane for the use of their lovely home.

The collection of garments were designed by Janet Biggs. Lavinia, Dulcie, Ivy, Morwenna, Lynnet and Elizabeth were based on ideas by Nina Shuttlewood. All yarns were designed and spun by Nina Shuttlewood.

Introduction

She seeketh wool, flax and worketh willingly with her hands.
(Proverbs 31:13)

The idea for this book came about because the spinner can never find knitting patterns for her own hand spun yarns. Although there are numerous books on spinning and spinning techniques, they do not contain sufficient information to enable the reader to create garments similar to those depicted. It is not sufficient to say 3oz Herdwick, 6oz Swaledale or whatever, without some indication of the thickness of the spun yarn required.

What we are introducing is a unique Chart called the Ross System which allows *all* knitters of both hand spun and commercial yarns to know instantly what yarns they are using or requiring to use on any of the following designs.

We are all thoroughly spoiled and to some extent brainwashed in the knitting world in that all spinners of commercial yarns such as Patons, Twilleys, Georges Picaud create their own designs around *only* their own yarns and we the knitters, are nervous of experimenting with either yarn or pattern; but to see some beautiful yarn in a shop and find that the corresponding patterns are not quite what we are looking for can be quite frustrating.

By using the Ross System all knitters using both hand spun and commercial yarns will easily be able to work out how many threads per cm (in) will be needed to arrive at the thickness of the yarn needed for the garment they intend to knit, and then cast on with confidence.

For example, if you wish to knit the sweater Jamesina (see p. 14) in a yarn other than the one suggested, by winding the threads around a pencil which has been marked out in centimetres (inches) for hand spinners you discover that the thickness of the yarn required will need to be 8 threads per cm or 20 threads per in. For any commercial yarn it must be 4.5 threads per cm or 11 threads per in. Looking across the chart, this tells us that the yarn is Aran type (thin) for which 4.5 metric or British number 7 needles are required. Therefore *any* commercial yarn that gives us 4.5 threads per centimetre or 11 threads to the inch between the pencilled marking can be used in conjunction with either 4.5 metric or British 7 knitting needles.

We have especially made a point of using straightforward spinning yarns throughout the book and have not used bouclés or slub or anything deliberately textured. All varieties of yarn have been obtained by varying the thickness, plying two different types of yarn or blending two or more different types of fibres together. Therefore there is no special skill required to produce each and every one of these designs, only a knowledge of spinning on either a spindle or a spinning wheel.

Hand spun is approximately just over half the weight of commercial yarn, so when using commercial yarns allow just a little more.

1 THE ROSS SYSTEM

To spin yarn for any particular pattern and produce the desired hand-knitted garment exactly it is essential that yarn be spun of the correct thickness. A simple method of measuring yarn thickness is illustrated below. (Figures 1 and 2.)

Spin a little yarn; now, pull back a length from the bobbin. Using a small rod or pencil wind the yarn round it for 2 cm (1 in), carefully observing the correct direction of winding as illustrated so the yarn is not untwisted as you wind it.

The successive circuits of the thread should lie close together, as shown, but not be packed forcibly.

Count the number of threads covering 2 cm or 1 in and you have a measure of the thread thickness. (If using metric measure cover a minimum of 2 cm and divide the resulting number of threads by 2 to arrive at the correct 'threads per centimetre' measure.)

If thread thickness is not as desired adjust as you spin, drawing out fibres further for a thinner thread giving more threads per inch (cm), or, for a thicker thread draw fibres out less. Once correct thickness is achieved break off a length of a good sample, tie in a loop (to keep the twist) and keep handy for reference.

Figure 1 Measuring the thread thickness for Z twist

Figure 2 Measuring the thread thickness for S twist

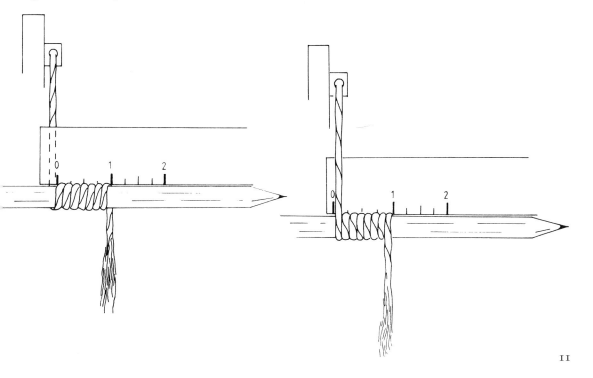

Table: The Ross System

1	2	3	4	5	6	7	8
Commercial yarn type			*Appropriate average knitting pin size*			*Required hand spun singles which when 2-plied will give equivalent to commercial*	
	No. of threads per in	*No. of threads per cm*	*British*	*Metric*	*American*	*No. of threads per in*	*No. of threads per cm*
2-ply fingering	25	10	13	2	0	45	18
3-ply fingering	19	7.5	12/11	2.5	1/2	35	14
4-ply fingering	16	6.5	10	3.0	3	27	11
Double Knitting (thin)	14	5.5	9	3.5	4	25	10
Double Knitting (thick)	12	5.0	8	4.0	5	22	9
Aran type (thin)	11	4.5	7	4.5	6	20	8
Aran type (thick)	10	4.0	6/5	5.0	7/8	17	7
Double-double	9	3.5	5/4	5.5/6.0	8/9	15	6
Chunky	7/8	3.0	3/2	6/7	10/10½	13	5.5
6-ply rug	5	2.0				9	3.5

The chart enables yarn similar to any commercial yarn to be spun by the hand-spinner. It lists, in Column 1 (the left-hand column) the main basic types of commercial yarns from '2-ply fingering' up to 'chunky'. Columns 2 and 3 give the approximate thickness of these yarns measured as 'threads per inch' and also 'threads per centimetre'.

Columns 4, 5 and 6 give the size of knitting needles (in British, metric and American sizing) commonly, though not invariably, used for that yarn. Finally columns 7 and 8 list the thickness (threads per inch and centimetre) of the singles yarn which should be spun, which, when it is 2-plyed will be similar in thickness to that of the corresponding commercial yarn.

NOTE

If you wish for a 3-ply yarn for any reason, then your singles will require to be *half* the thickness of the final yarn required.

2 PURE WOOL

It is important when choosing your pattern to use the right type of wool or fleece for the garment you intend to make. The British Wool Marketing Board sort their fleece into three categories:

1 Mountain and Hill
2 Longwool and Lustre
3 Shortwool and Down

Mountain and Hill, as far as knitting is concerned, is used mostly for outer garments as the fleece is somewhat coarse but very hardwearing.

Longwool and Lustre is equally as hardwearing but much softer.

Shortwool and Down is very fine soft fleece suitable for all garments worn next to the skin, such as baby clothes, sweaters, shawls, etc.

Therefore, if you are planning to knit a coat which will require a lot of exposure to the weather, then it is important to choose a Mountain and Hill breed first and perhaps a Longwool and Lustre breed second. Not a Shortwool and Down. Alternatively, if you are wanting a soft-feeling garment, like a sweater, camisole, matinée coat, etc., then use the Shortwool and Down breed.

Another way of distinguishing the different categories of wool is by the 'Bradford Count' which is a numerical count system to find the technical classification of wool in terms of fibre diameter. This count refers to the number of 'hanks' of yarn, each 560 yards long, which can be spun from one pound of wool top. Thus a 64s wool would yield 35,840 yards (560 yards times 64).

Whilst the sheep or wool of Britain, United States and most other countries are graded under the 'Bradford Count', there is also a growing effort in the United States to institute the use of the 'micron system', which is a substantially more technical and accurate measurement to determine the fineness of the average diameter of wool fibre in a given lot of wool. The micron (1/35,000 of an inch) is used as the actual average diameter measurement. For example, an 80s wool which averages 18.1 microns, is less than one half the average diameter of a Common and Braid 36s which has an average diameter of 39.7 microns.

You will see under the British Mountain and Hill and the American Longwool Breeds the numbers under the Bradford Count range from the 28s to 56s: under the Longwool and Lustre and Medium Wool Breeds 44s to 54s and lastly under the Shortwool and Down and the Finewool/Crossbreeds Wools 54s to 80s. Therefore the smaller the count the coarser the breed and so on.

Listed on the next page are some breeds to try under the British and American headings, with the Bradford Count alongside.

Bradford Count of British and American Breeds

BRITISH

Mountain and Hill
Herdwick 28s–32s
Swaledale 28s–40s
Welsh 36s–50s
Scottish Blackface 46s–48s
Cheviot 48s–56s

Longwool and Lustre
Romney Marsh 48s–54s
Wensleydale 44s–48s
Border Leicester 44s–48s
Lincoln Longwool 36s–40s
Leicester Longwool 48s–50s

Shortwool and Down
Shetland 56s–60s
Jacob 44s–56s
Suffolk 54s–58s
Dorset Down 56s–58s
Ryeland 56s–58s
Kerry Hill 54s–56s

AMERICAN

Longwool Breeds
Lincoln 36s–46s
Cotswold 36s–40s
Romney 40s–48s

Medium Wool Breeds
Southdown 56s–60s
Suffolk 48s–56s
Oxford 46s–50s
Cheviot 48s–56s
Dorset 48s–56s

Fine Wool
American, or Delaine-Merino 64s–80s
Rambouillet 62s–70s

Crossbreed Wool Breeds
Corriedale 50s–60s
Targhee 58s–60s
Romeldale 58s–60s
Columbia 50s–60s

Jamesina

Breed: Jacob
Category: Shortwool and Down

A simple dropped-shoulder, slash-neck sweater done in the very popular Jacob yarn. The dramatic effect has been obtained by using a cunningly simple pattern and striping in four colour combinations from the same fleece.

COMBINATION

Two strands of black, plyed together.
Two strands of white, plyed together.
One strand of black, one strand of white, plyed together.
Black/white random carded, plyed together.

MATERIALS

Hand Spun – Jacob
8 threads per cm – Single ply
20 threads per in – Single ply

Commercial Equivalent – Aran type (thin)
4.5 threads per cm
11 threads per in

100(110:125)g of Main Shade (Black and White carded together).
115(125:140)g of A (White).
85(95:105)g of B (Single-ply Black and Single-ply White – plyed together).
85(95:105)g of C (Black).

1 Jamesina

Pair each 3¾mm and 4½mm knitting needles.
NB If using a commercial yarn allow extra.

MEASUREMENTS

To fit bust 76–81(86–91:97–102)cm
  [30–32(34–36:38–40)in].
Length from top of shoulders 55(56:57)cm
  [21¾(22:22½)in].
Sleeve seam 46cm [18in].

TENSION

On 4½mm needles, 24 sts to 10cm [4in] measured
over pattern, 40 rows (1 pattern repeat) = 16cm
[6¼in].

BACK AND FRONT (Alike)

With 3¾mm needles and MS, cast on 102(112:
  124)sts and work in K1, P1 rib for 7cm [2¾in], inc
  0(1:0)st at end of last row. [102(113:124)sts]
Change to 4½mm needles and work in patt as folls:
1st row In MS, K2, yfwd, K1, yfwd, *[sl1, K1,
  psso] twice, [K2tog] twice, yfwd, [K1, yfwd] 3
  times; rep from * to last 11 sts [sl1, K1, psso]
  twice, [K2tog] twice, yfwd, K1, yfwd, K2.
2nd row In MS, P.
3rd–6th rows Rep last 2 rows twice more.
7th–10th rows In A, rep 1st and 2nd rows twice.
11th row In B, as 1st.
12th row In B, K.
13th row In C, as 1st.
14th row In C, K.
15th and 16th rows In B, as 11th and 12th.
17th–20th rows In C, rep 1st and 2nd rows twice.
21st row In MS, as 1st.
22nd row In MS, K.
23rd and 24th rows In A, as 1st and 2nd.
25th and 26th rows In MS, as 1st and 2nd.

27th and 28th rows In A, as 1st and 2nd.
29th–32nd rows In B, rep 1st and 2nd rows twice.
33rd row In C, as 1st.
34th row In C, K.
35th–38th rows In A, rep 1st and 2nd rows twice.
39th row In C, as 1st.
40th row In C, K.
These 40 rows form patt.
Work straight in patt until Back measures 36cm
  [14¼in], ending with r.s. facing.
Shape armholes by casting off 11 sts at beg of next
  2 rows [80(91:102)sts]
Cont in patt until armhole measures 17(18:19)cm
  [6¾(7:7½)in], ending with r.s. facing.
Change to 3¾mm needles and cont in g.st. (every
  row K), for 2cm [¾in], ending with w.s. facing.
Cast off.

SLEEVES

With 3¾mm needles and MS, cast on 50(54:54)sts
  and work in K1, P1 rib for 6cm [2¼in].
Next row Rib 5(3:3), M1, [rib 1, M1], 40(47:47)
  times, rib 5(4:4). [91(102:102)sts]
Change to 4½mm needles and work in patt as given
  for Back until sleeve seam measures 46cm [18in],
  ending with r.s. facing.
Place markers at each end of last row.
Work straight for a further 4.5cm [1¾in], ending
  with r.s. facing. Cast off.

MAKE UP

Leaving a gap of 22cm [8¾in] for head, join
  shoulders.
Placing centre of sleeve to shoulder, sew in sleeves
  between markers.
Join side and sleeve seams.
Press lightly on wrong side.

Guinevere

Breed: Shetland
Category: Shortwool and Down

A lovely w~dding dress which has been knitted in finely spun white Shetland which has been combed instead of carded. The skirt has wide lace panels of a delicate openwork of diamonds. The whole of the bodice and sleeves have been threaded alternatively with cream, beige and peach ribbons and allowed to flow freely from the waist ending with tiny rosettes, using all three shades of ribbons. The rosettes are also added to each sleeve, cuff and neck.

MATERIALS

Hand Spun – Shetland
10 threads per cm – Single ply
25 threads per in – Single ply

Commercial Equivalent – Double Knitting (thin)
5.5 threads per cm
14 threads per in
800(850:900:950)g of Combed Shetland Wool.
Pair each 3mm and 4mm knitting needles.
38(40:42:44) metres of narrow ribbon in contrasting colours.
Length of elastic for waist.
NB If using a commercial yarn allow extra.

MEASUREMENTS

To fit bust 81(86:91:97)cm [32(34:36:38)in].
Length from top of shoulders approx 142(145: 146:148)cm [56(57:57½:58¼)in] allowing for blousing at waist.
Sleeve seam 46cm [18in].

TENSION

25 sts and 32 rows to 10cm [4in] measured over stocking stitch on 4mm needles.

LACE PANEL (15 sts)

When working lace panel on skirt, you may find it useful to mark panels with markers to ensure correct working.

1st row K4, K2tog, yfwd, K2, K2tog, yfwd, K3, yfwd, sl1, K1, psso.
2nd and every alt row P.
3rd row K3, K2tog, yfwd [K1, yfwd, sl1, K1, psso] twice, K1, K2tog, yfwd, K1.
5th row K2, K2tog, yfwd, K3, yfwd, sl1, K1, psso, K1, yfwd, K3tog, yfwd, K2.
7th row K1, K2tog, yfwd, K1, yfwd, sl1, K1, psso, K2, yfwd, sl1, K1, psso, K2tog, yfwd, K3.
9th row K2tog, yfwd, K3, yfwd, sl1, K1, psso, K2, yfwd, sl1, K1, psso, K4.
11th row K1, yfwd, sl1, K1, psso [K1, K2tog, yfwd] twice, K1, yfwd, sl1, K1, psso, K3.
13th row K2, yfwd, sl1, K2tog, psso, yfwd, K1, K2tog, yfwd, K3, yfwd, sl1, K1, psso, K2.
15th row K3, yfwd, sl1, K1, psso, K2tog, yfwd, K2, K2tog, yfwd, K1, yfwd, sl1, K1, psso, K1.
16th row As 2nd.
These 16 rows form Lace Panel.

BACK

**With 3mm needles, cast on 210(222:243:255)sts and work in g.st. for 11 rows.
Change to 4mm needles and work in st.st. placing lace panels as folls:
1st row K10(11:14:15) [Lace Panel as 1st row, K20(22:25:27)] 5 times, Lace Panel as 1st row, K10(11:14:15).
2nd row P10(11:14:15) [Lace Panel as 2nd row, P20(22:25:27)] 5 times, Lace Panel as 2nd row, P10(11:14:15).
Cont thus working appropriate rows of lace panel until work measures 44(44:36:36)cm [17¼(17¼: 14¼:14¼)in], ending with r.s. facing.
Shape skirt as folls:
Next row K8(9:12:13), K2tog [Lace Panel 15 sts, K2togtbl, K16(18:21:23), K2tog] 5 times, Lace Panel 15 sts, K2togtbl, K8(9:12:13). [198(210: 231:243)sts]
Work 31 rows.
Keeping panels correct, cont dec on r.s. as before on next and every 32nd row until 150(162:171: 183)sts rem.

2 Guinevere

Work straight until skirt section measures 98(99: 99:100)cm [38½(39:39:39¼)in] ending with w.s. facing.

Adjust skirt length here if necessary.

Next row *P1, P2tog; rep from * to end. [100(108:114:122)sts]

Change to 3mm needles and work 7 rows in K1, P1, rib.

Next row Rib 6 (9:5:7), M1, [rib 11(15:13:18), M1] 8(6:8:6) times, rib to end. [109(115: 123:129)sts]

Change to 4mm needles and work in patt for bodice as folls:

1st row K18(16:20:23) [K1, yfwd, sl1, K1, psso, K2, K2tog, yfwd, K3] 7(8:8:8) times, K1, yfwd, sl1, K1, psso, K18(16:20:23).

2nd and every alt row P.

3rd row K18(16:20:23) [K1, yfwd, sl1, K1, psso, K1, K2tog, yfwd, K1, yfwd, sl1, K1, psso, K1] 7(8:8:8) times, K1, yfwd, sl1, K1, psso, K18(16: 20:23).

5th row K18(16:20:23) [K1, yfwd, sl1, K1, psso, K2tog, yfwd, K3, yfwd, sl1, K1, psso] 7(8:8:8) times, K1, yfwd, sl1, K1, psso, K18(16:20:23).

7th row K18(16:20:23) [K1, yfwd, sl1, K1, psso, K1, yfwd, sl1, K1, psso, K1, K2tog, yfwd, K1] 7(8:8:8) times, K1, yfwd, sl1, K1, psso, K18(16: 20:23).

9th row K18(16:20:23) [K1, yfwd, sl1, K1, psso, K2, yfwd, sl1, K2tog, psso, yfwd, K2] 7(8:8:8) times, K1, yfwd, sl1, K1, psso, K18(16:20:23).

10th row As 2nd.

These 10 rows form patt for bodice.

Work straight in patt until Back Bodice measures 25(26:26:26)cm [9¾(10¼:10¼:10¼)]in, from beginning of waist ribbing, ending with r.s. facing.

Keeping patt correct, *shape armholes* by casting off 4(5:5:5)sts at beg of next 2 rows.

Dec 1 st at each end of next 3(3:5:7) rows, then on every alt row until 81(85:87:91)sts rem.**

Work straight until armhole measures 19(20:21: 22)cm [7½(8:8¼:8¾)in], ending with r.s. facing.

Shape shoulders by casting off 8 sts at beg of next 4 rows, then 7(8:8:8)sts at beg of foll 2 rows.

Leave rem 35(37:39:43)sts on a spare needle.

FRONT

Work as for Back from ** to **.

Work straight until armhole measures 12(13:14: 15)cm [4¾(5¼:5½:6)in], ending with r.s. facing.

Keeping patt correct, *divide for neck* as folls:

Next row Patt 30(32:32:34), K2tog, turn and leave rem sts on a spare needle.

Dec 1 st at neck edge on every row until 23(24: 24:24)sts rem.

Work straight until Front matches Back to shoulder, ending with r.s. facing.

Shape shoulder by casting off 8 sts at beg of next and foll alt row. Work 1 row. Cast off rem 7(8:8:8)sts.

With r.s. facing, slip centre 17(17:19:19)sts on a spare needle, rejoin yarn to rem sts, K2tog, patt to end.

Work to match first side, reversing shapings.

SLEEVES

With 3mm needles, cast on 54(56:56:58)sts and work in K1, P1 rib for 3cm [1¼in].

Next row *Rib 1, M1; rep from * to last st, rib 1. [107(111:111:115)sts]

Change to 4mm needles and work in patt as folls:

1st row K2(4:4:1), *K1, yfwd, sl1, K1, psso, K2, K2tog, yfwd, K3; rep from * to last 5(7:7:4)sts, K1, yfwd, sl1, K1, psso, K2(4:4:1).

2nd and every alt row P.

3rd row K2(4:4:1), *K1, yfwd, sl1, K1, psso, K1, K2tog, yfwd, K1, yfwd, sl1, K1, psso, K1; rep from * to last 5(5:5:4)sts, K1, yfwd, sl1, K1, psso, K2(4:4:1).

5th row K2(4:4:1), *K1, yfwd, sl1, K1, psso, K2tog, yfwd, K3, yfwd, sl1, K1, psso; rep from * to last 5(7:7:4)sts, K1, yfwd, sl1, K1, psso, K2(4:4:1).

7th row K2(4:4:1), *K1, yfwd, sl1, K1, psso, K1, yfwd, sl1, K1, psso, K1, K2tog, yfwd, K1; rep from * to last 5(7:7:4)sts, K1, yfwd, sl1, K1, psso, K2(4:4:1).

9th row K2(4:4:1), *K1, yfwd, sl1, K1, psso, K2, yfwd, sl1, K2tog, psso, yfwd, K2; rep from * to last 5(7:7:4)sts, K1, yfwd, sl1, K1, psso, K2(4:4:1).

10th row As 2nd.

These 10 rows form patt for sleeves.

Work straight until sleeve measures 46cm [18in], ending with r.s. facing.

Keeping patt correct, *shape top* by casting off 4(5:5:5)sts at beg of next 2 rows.

Dec 1 st at each end of next and every foll alt row until 63(59:51:51)sts rem.

1ST AND 2ND SIZES

Dec 1 st at each end of every row until 51 sts rem.

ALL SIZES

Cast off rem sts.

MAKE UP AND NECK BORDER

Press lightly on w.s. using a damp cloth and warm iron.

Join right shoulder seam.

Neck Border

With r.s. facing, 3mm needles, *Knit up* 19 sts down left side of neck, K17(17:19:19)sts from front, *Knit up* 19 sts up right side of neck, K35(37:39: 43)sts from back. [90(92:96:100)sts]

Work in K1, P1 rib for 4cm [1½in].

Using a 4mm needle, cast off loosely in rib.

Join left shoulder and Neck Border.

Fold Neck Border in half to w.s. and slip hem loosely in position.

Join side and sleeve seams.

Gather sleeve head and insert sleeves.

Join elastic for waist into a circle and placing at waist ribbing, herringbone in position.

Thread ribbons through eyelets on bodice as in photograph, thread behind waist ribbing and through to r.s. and leaving hanging free.

Thread ribbons on sleeve as illustrated.

Make rosettes with ribbons, of varying sizes and colours and attach to wrists, neckline and ends of free hanging ribbons.

To make a rosette: With a length of ribbon and threaded needle, run a gathering thread through ribbon, draw up tightly to form rosette, secure neatly.

Cheryl

Breed: Cheviot
Category: Mountain and Hill

A pretty little waistcoat which can be spun in almost any yarn and threaded with matching ribbons through the eyelet holes between the lacey cables.

MATERIALS

Hand Spun – Cheviot
9 threads per cm – Single ply
22 threads per in – Single ply

Commercial Equivalent – Double Knitting (thick)
5 threads per cm
12 threads per in
200(225:250:275)g of Cheviot.
Pair each 3¼mm and 4mm knitting needles.
3 metres of narrow ribbon for all sizes.
7 horn buttons.
NB If using a commercial yarn allow extra.

MEASUREMENTS

To fit bust 86(91:97:102)cm [34(36:38:40)in].
Length from top of shoulders 56(57:58:60)cm [22(22½:22¾:23½)in].

TENSION

22 sts and 30 rows to 10cm [4in] measured over stocking stitch on 4mm needles.
Panel Pattern measures 10cm [4in].

SPECIAL ABBREVIATIONS

Tw2 = Twist 2 by knitting together next 2 sts through back of loops, then before slipping sts off needle, K into back of first st again.
C7F = slip next 2 sts onto cable needle and leave at front of work, Tw2, yfwd, sl1, K2tog, psso, yfwd, then Tw2 from cable needle.

PANEL PATTERN (26 sts)

1st row Yrn, P2tog [P1, Tw2, yfwd, sl1, K2tog, psso, yfwd, Tw2, P2, yrn, P2tog] twice.
2nd and every alt row K4, P7, K5, P7, K3.
3rd, 7th and 11th rows P3, Tw2, yfwd, sl1, K2tog, psso, yfwd, Tw2, P5, Tw2, yfwd, sl1, K2tog, psso, yfwd, Tw2, P4.
5th row Yrn, P2tog [P1, C7F, P2, yrn, P2tog] twice.
9th row As 1st.
12th row As 2nd.
These 12 rows form panel patt.

BACK

With 3¼mm needles, cast on 90(96:102:108)sts and work in K1, P1 rib for 6cm [2¼in].
Next row Rib 7(8:8:9), M1, [rib 15(16:17:18), M1] 5 times, rib to end. [96(102:108:114)sts]
Change to 4mm needles and starting with a K row, work in st.st until Back measures 36cm [14¼in], ending with a P row.
Shape armholes by casting off 3(3:4:4)sts at beg of next 2 rows, then dec 1 st at each end of next 3(5:5:5) rows, then on every foll alt row until 72(76:80:82)sts rem.
Work straight until armhole measures 20(21:22:24)cm [8(8¼:8¾:9½)in], ending with r.s. facing.
Shape shoulders by casting off 6(7:7:7)sts at beg of next 4 rows, then 7(6:7:7)sts at beg of foll 2 rows.
Leave rem 34(36:38:40)sts on a spare needle.

LEFT FRONT

**With 3¼mm needles, cast on 46(48:52:54)sts and work in K1, P1 rib for 6cm [2¼in].
Next row Rib 3(3:4:3), M1, [rib 8(7:9:8), M1] 5(6:5:6) times, rib to end. [52(55:58:61)sts]**
Change to 4mm needles and *place panel* as folls:
1st row K24(27:30:33), Panel Patt 26 sts as 1st row, K2.
2nd row P2, Panel Patt 26 sts as 2nd row, P to end.
Cont thus working appropriate rows of panel patt, until Front matches Back to armhole, ending with r.s. facing.
Shape armhole, keeping panel patt correct, by casting off 3(3:4:4)sts at beg of next row. Work 1 row.

3 Cheryl

Dec 1 st at armhole edge on next 3(5:5:5) rows, then on every alt row until 40(42:44:45) sts rem.

Work straight until armhole measures 12(13:14: 15)cm [4¾(5¼:5½:6)in], ending with r.s. facing.

Shape front neck as folls:

Next row Patt 32(33:34:35), K2tog, turn and leave rem 6(7:8:8)sts on a spare needle.

Cont on these sts, dec 1 st at neck edge of every row until 19(20:21:21)sts rem. Work a few rows straight until Front matches Back to shoulder, ending with r.s. facing.

Shape shoulder by casting off 6(7:7:7)sts at beg of next and foll alt row. Work 1 row.

Cast off rem 7(6:7:7)sts.

RIGHT FRONT

Work as for Left Front from ** to **.

Change to 4mm needles and *place panel patt* as folls:

1st row K2, Panel Patt 26 sts as 1 st row, K to end.

2nd row P24(27:30:33)sts, Panel Patt 26 sts as 2nd row, P2.

Cont thus, complete as given for Left Front, reversing shapings.

MAKE UP AND BORDERS

Join shoulders.

Neck Border

With 3¼mm needles, r.s. facing and starting at right front neck, K6(7:8:8)sts from spare needle, *Knit up* 18(18:18:20)sts up right side of neck to shoulder, K34(36:38:40)sts from back inc 1 st at centre, *Knit up* 18(18:18:20)sts down left side of neck, K6(7:8:8)sts from spare needle. [83(87:91: 97)sts]

Work in K1, P1 rib (rows on r.s. having a K1 at each end), for 9 rows.

Cast off in rib.

Buttonhole Border

With r.s. facing, 3¼mm needles, starting at lower edge of right front, *Knit up* 111(117:117:119)sts to top of Neck Border.

1st row K1, *P1, K1; rep from * to end.

2nd row K2, *P1, K1; rep from * to last st, K1.

Rep 1st row once more.

Buttonhole row Rib 4(4:4:5), *cast off 2 sts, rib 15(16:16:16) including st on needle after cast off; rep from * to last 5(5:5:6)sts, cast off 2, rib to end.

Next row Rib, casting on 2 sts over those cast off.

Work 4 more rows in rib as given.

Cast off evenly in rib.

Button Border

With r.s. facing, 3¼mm needles, starting at top of Neck Border on Left Front, *Knit up* 111(117: 117:119)sts down left front.

Work 9 rows in rib as given for Buttonhole Border.

Cast off in rib.

Armhole Borders

With 3¼mm needles and r.s. facing, *Knit up* 88(92:96:106)sts all round armhole.

Work 9 rows in K1, P1 rib.

Cast off evenly in rib.

Join side seams and armhole borders.

Thread ribbons through eyelets on Fronts and secure on w.s.

Press seam.

Sew on buttons.

Joanna

Breed: Jacob
Category: Shortwool and Down

A fascinating stole which has been given a delicate allure by using two strands of **unplyed** yarn together throughout coupled with a clever colour change.

COMBINATION

Two strands of Black.
Two strands of White.
Two strands of random carded.

MATERIALS

Hand Spun – Jacob
14 threads per cm – Single ply
35 threads per in – Single ply

Commercial Equivalent – Three-ply
fingering
7.5 threads per cm
19 threads per in
100g of Main Shade, 50g of 1st Contrast and 50g of 2nd Contrast.
Pair 4½mm knitting needles.
NB If using a commercial yarn allow extra.

MEASUREMENTS

Width approx 53cm [21in].
Length approx 151cm [60in].

TENSION

18 sts and 23 rows to 10cm [4in] measured over pattern on 4½mm needles.

SPECIAL ABBREVIATIONS

MS = Main Shade; A = 1st Contrast; B = 2nd Contrast.
NB Two single plys of Jacob are used together throughout.

STOLE

With 4½mm needles and MS, cast on 96 sts and K1 row.
Work in patt as folls:
1st row In MS, K.
2nd row In MS, *K6, yfwd, yrn, K1, yfwd, [yrn] twice, K1, yfwd, [yrn] 3 times, K1, yfwd, [yrn] twice, K1, yfwd, yrn, K6; rep from * to end.
3rd row In MS, K dropping all the yfwds and yrns off needle.
4th row In MS, K.
5th row In A, K.
6th row In A, K1, rep from * of 2nd row, ending last rep with K1 instead of K6.
7th row In A, as 3rd.
8th row In A, K.
9th–12th rows In MS, as 1st–4th.
13th–16th rows In B, as 5th–8th.
These 16 rows form patt.
Work straight in patt until stole measures approx 151cm [60in], ending with 12th row of patt. Cast off.
Block and press stole.

4 Joanna

Kirsty

Breed: Shetland
Category: Shortwool and Down

This attractive lace and ribboned sweater in pale grey Shetland can be worn on any occasion. Equally charming with or without ribbons.

MATERIALS

Hand Spun – Shetland
7 threads per cm – Single ply
17 threads per in – Single ply

Commercial Equivalent – Aran Type Thick
4 threads per cm
10 threads per in
475(500:550:600)g of Shetland.
Pair each 4mm and 5mm knitting needles.
Circular 4mm and 5mm needles.
3.10(3.10:3.50:3.90) metres of Main Shade of Ribbon.
2.20(2.20:2.60:3.00) metres of Contrast Ribbon.
NB If using a commercial yarn allow extra.

MEASUREMENTS

To fit chest 81(86:91:97)cm [32(34:36:38)in].
Length from top of shoulders 60(61:62:63)cm [23¾(24:24½:24¾)in].
Sleeve seam 46(46:47:47)cm [18(18:18½:18½)in].

TENSION

18 sts and 24 rows to 10cm [4in] measured over stocking stitch on 5mm needles.

BACK

**With 4mm needles, cast on 72(78:82:88)sts and work in K1, P1 rib for 6cm [2¼in].
Next row Rib 4(4:6:5), M1, [rib 9(10:10:11), M1] 7 times, rib 5(4:6:6). [80(86:90:96)sts].
Change to 5mm needles and starting with a K row, work in st.st until Back measures 38cm [15in], ending with a P row.**
Shape armholes by casting off 4(4:5:5)sts at beg of next 2 rows.

1ST, 3RD AND 4TH SIZES
Dec 1 st at each end of next row. Work 3 rows.
Rep last 4 rows 0(2:2) times more.

1ST, 2ND AND 4TH SIZES
Dec 1 st at each end of next row. Work 1 row.
Rep last 2 rows 0(3:0) times more.

ALL SIZES
Leave rem 68(70:74:78)sts on a spare needle.

FRONT

Work as for Back from ** to **.
Shape armholes and *divide for neck* as follows:

1ST SIZE
1st row Cast off 4, K21 (including st on needle after cast off), turn and leave rem sts on a spare needle.
2nd and every alt row Sl1, P to end.
3rd row K2tog, K13, turn.
5th row K8, turn.
7th row K2tog, K2, turn.
8th row Sl1, P to end.
Slip 19 sts of side neck on a length of yarn.

2ND, 3RD AND 4TH SIZES
Cast off (4(5:5)sts at beg of next 2 rows.

3RD AND 4TH SIZES
Dec 1 st at each end of next row. Work 3 rows.

4TH SIZE
Dec 1 st at each end of next row. Work 1 row.

2ND, 3RD AND 4TH SIZES
Divide for neck as folls:
1st row [K2tog] 1(1:0) time, K22(22:26), turn and leave rem sts on a spare needle.
2nd and every alt row Sl1, P to end.
3rd row [K2tog] 1(0:1) time, K15(17:18), turn.
5th row [K2tog] 1(1:0) time, K8(9:11), turn.
7th row [K2tog] 1(0:1) time, K3(4:4), turn.
8th row Sl1, P to end.
Slip 20(22:24)sts of side neck on a length of yarn.

ALL SIZES
With r.s. facing, slip centre 30 sts on a length of yarn, rejoin yarn to rem sts and complete to match first side, reversing shapings.

5 Kirsty

SLEEVES

With 4mm needles, cast on 40(42:42:44)sts and work in K1, P1 rib for 6cm [2¼in].

Next row Rib 5(6:6:5), M1, [rib 10(10:10:11), M1] 3 times, rib 5(6:6:6). [44(46:46:48)sts].

Change to 5mm needles and starting with a K row, work in st.st *shaping sides* by inc 1 st at each end of 3rd and every foll 8th row until there are 64(66:68:70)sts.

Work straight until sleeve seam measures 46(46:
47:47)cm [18(18:18½:18½)in], ending with a P
row.
Shape armholes by casting off 4(4:5:5)sts at beg of
next 2 rows.

1ST, 3RD AND 4TH SIZES
Dec 1 st at each end of next row. Work 3 rows.
Rep last 4 rows 0(2:2) times more.

1ST, 2ND AND 4TH SIZES
Dec 1 st at each end of next row. Work 1 row. Rep
last 2 rows 0(3:0) times more

ALL SIZES
Leave rem 52(50:52:54)sts on a spare needle.

YOKE

With r.s. facing, slip 34(35:37:39)sts of Back onto
a spare needle.
With circular 5mm needle, starting at centre of
back, K34(35:37:39)sts from back, 52(50:52:
54)sts from sleeve, 68(70:74:78)sts from front,
52(50:52:54)sts from right sleeve, 34(35:37:39)
sts from back. Mark beg of rounds. [240(240:
252:264)sts].
1st round K.
2nd round P.
3rd round *Yfwd, K2tog; rep from * to end.
4th round P.
5th round *K1, yfwd, sl1, K1, psso, K7, K2tog,
yfwd; rep from * to end.
6th, 8th, 10th, 12th and 14th rounds K.
7th round *K2, yfwd, sl1, K1, psso, K5, K2tog,
yfwd, K1; rep from * to end.
9th round *K3, yfwd, sl1, K1, psso, K3, K2tog,
yfwd, K2; rep from * to end.
11th round *K4, yfwd, sl1, K1, psso, K1, K2tog,
yfwd, K3; rep from * to end.
13th round *K5, yfwd, sl1, K2tog, psso, yfwd, K4;
rep from * to end.
15th round *K1, K2tog, K7, K2tog; rep from * to
end.
16th round P.
17th round As 3rd.
18th round P.
19th round *K1, yfwd, sl1, K1, psso, K5, K2tog,
yfwd; rep from * to end.

20th, 22nd, 24th and 26th rounds K.
21st round *K2, yfwd, sl1, K1, psso, K3, K2tog,
yfwd, K1; rep from * to end.
23rd round *K3, yfwd, sl1, K1, psso, K1, K2tog,
yfwd, K2; rep from * to end.
25th round *K4, yfwd, sl1, K2tog, psso, yfwd, K3;
rep from * to end.
27th round *K1, K2tog, K5, K2tog; rep from * to
end.
28th round P.
29th round As 3rd.
30th round P.
31st round *K1, yfwd, sl1, K1, psso, K3, K2tog,
yfwd; rep from * to end.
32nd, 34th and 36th rounds K.
33rd round *K2, yfwd, sl1, K1, psso, K1, K2tog,
yfwd, K1; rep from * to end.
35th round *K3, yfwd, sl1, K2tog, psso, yfwd, K2;
rep from * to end.
37th round *K1, K2tog, K3, K2tog; rep from * to
end.
38th round P.
39th round As 3rd.
40th round P.
41st round *K1, yfwd, sl1, K1, psso, K1, K2tog,
yfwd; rep from * to end.
42nd and 44th rounds K.
43rd round *K2, yfwd, sl1, K2tog, psso, yfwd, K1;
rep from * to end.
45th round *K1, K2tog; rep from * to end.
46th round P.
47th round As 3rd.
48th round P.
[80(80:84:88)sts]
Change to 4mm circular needle and work in K1, P1
rib for 9cm [3½in].
Using a 5mm needle, cast off loosely in rib.
Fold Neck Border in half to wrong side and slip
hem loosely in position.
Join semi-armholes.
Join side and sleeve seams.
Press seams.
Thread ribbons through eyelets and fasten in
position.

Lavinia

Breed: Shetland
Category: Shortwool and Down

This classic design in Shetland moorit (moor rit = more red than brown) features horseshoe lace panels on centre front, back and sleeves, which can be trimmed either with or without contrasting ribbons.

MATERIALS

Hand Spun – Shetland
7 threads per cm – Single ply
17 threads per in – Single ply

Commercial Equivalent – Aran type (thick)
4 threads per cm
10 threads per in

475(500:525:550:575)g of Shetland.
Pair each 4mm and 5mm knitting needles.
6.5(6.5:7:7:7.5) metres of contrasting ribbon.
NB If using a commercial yarn allow extra.

MEASUREMENTS

To fit bust 81(86:91:97:102)cm [32(34:36:38:40)in].
Length from top of shoulder 55(56:57:58:60)cm [21$\frac{3}{4}$(22:22$\frac{1}{2}$:22$\frac{3}{4}$:23$\frac{3}{4}$)in].
Sleeve seam 44cm [17$\frac{1}{2}$in].

TENSION

18 sts and 22 rows to 10cm [4in], measured over stocking stitch on 5mm needles.

PANEL PATTERN A (38 sts)

1st row Yfwd, K2tog, *yfwd, K3, sl1, K2tog, psso, K3, yfwd, K1, yfwd, K2tog; rep from * twice more.
2nd and every alt row P.
3rd row K3, * yfwd, K2, sl1, K2tog, psso, K2, yfwd, K5; rep from * once more, yfwd, K2, sl1, K2tog, psso, K2, yfwd, K4.
5th row Yfwd, K2tog, * K2, yfwd, K1, sl1, K2tog, psso, K1, yfwd, K3, yfwd, K2tog; rep from * twice more.
7th row K5, * yfwd, sl1, K2tog, psso, yfwd, K9; rep from * once more, yfwd, sl1, K2tog, psso, yfwd, K6.
8th row As 2nd.
These 8 rows form panel patt A.

PANEL PATTERN B (14 sts)

1st row Yfwd, K2tog, yfwd, K3, sl1, K2tog, psso, K3, yfwd, K1, yfwd, K2tog.
2nd and every alt row P.
3rd row K3, yfwd, K2, sl1, K2tog, psso, K2, yfwd, K4.
5th row Yfwd, K2tog, K2, yfwd, K1, sl1, K2tog, psso, K1, yfwd, K3, yfwd, K2tog.
7th row K5, yfwd, sl1, K2tog, psso, yfwd, K6.
8th row As 2nd.
These 8 rows form panel patt B.

BACK

**With 4mm needles, cast on 72(76:82:86:90)sts and work in K1, P1 for 6cm [2$\frac{1}{4}$in].
Next row Rib 6(6:6:8:8), M1, [rib 12(13:14:14:15), M1] 5 times, rib to end. [78(82:88:92:96)sts]
Change to 5mm needles and work as folls:
1st row K20(22:25:27:29), Panel Patt A as 1st row, K to end.
2nd row P20(22:25:27:29), Panel Patt A as 2nd row, P to end.
Cont thus working appropriate rows of panel patt until Back measures 34cm [13$\frac{1}{4}$in] ending with r.s. facing.
Shape armholes, keeping panel correct, by casting off 3(3:4:4:4)sts at beg of next 2 rows, then dec 1 st at each end of next 3(3:3:5:5) rows, then on every alt row until 60(62:64:66:68)sts rem.**
Work straight until back measures 55(56:57:58:60)cm [21$\frac{3}{4}$(22:22$\frac{1}{2}$:22$\frac{3}{4}$:23$\frac{3}{4}$)in], ending with r.s. facing.
Shape shoulders by casting off 6 sts at beg of next 4 rows, then 5(5:6:6:6)sts at beg of foll 2 rows.
Leave rem 26(28:28:30:32)sts on a spare needle.

FRONT

Work as for Back from ** to **.

Work straight until Front matches Back to shoulder less 16(16:16:16:18) rows, thus ending with r.s. facing.

Divide for neck, keeping panel correct, as folls:

Next row Patt 22(22:23:24:24), K2tog, turn and leave rem sts on a spare needle.

Cont on these sts for first side, dec 1 st at neck edge on every row until 17(17:18:18:18)sts rem.

Work a few rows straight until Front matches Back to shoulder, ending with r.s. facing.

Shape shoulder by casting off 6 sts at beg of next and foll alt row. Work 1 row. Cast off rem 5(5:6:6:6)sts.

With r.s. facing, slip centre 12(14:14:14:16)sts on a spare needle, rejoin yarn to rem sts, K2tog, patt to end.

Work to match first side, reversing shapings.

SLEEVES

With 4mm needles, cast on 40(42:42:44:44)sts and work in K1, P1 rib for 8cm [3¼in].

Next row Rib 5(4:4:5:5), M1, [rib 10(11:11:11:11), M1] 3 times, rib to end. [44(46:46:48:48)sts]

Change to 5mm needles and work as folls:

1st row K15(16:16:17:17), Panel Patt B as 1st row, K to end.

2nd row P15(16:16:17:17), Panel Patt B as 2nd row, P to end.

Cont thus working appropriate rows of panel patt, *shaping sides* by inc 1 st at each end of 3rd

and every foll 10th row until there are 50(52:54:56:58)sts.

Work straight until sleeve seam measures 44cm [17½in], ending with r.s. facing.

Shape top, keeping panel correct, by casting off 3(3:4:4:4)sts at beg of next 2 rows.

Dec 1 st at each end of next row. Work 3 rows.

Rep last 4 rows 3(3:4:4:5) times more. [36(38:36:38:38)sts]

Dec 1 st at each end of next and every foll alt row until 18 sts rem, ending with r.s. facing.

Cast off rem sts.

MAKE UP AND NECK BORDER

Press lightly on w.s.

Join right shoulder seam.

Neck Border With 4mm needles, r.s. facing, starting at left shoulder, *Knit up* 13(13:13:13:15)sts down left side of neck, K12(14:14:14:16)sts from front, *Knit up* 13(13:13:13:15)sts up right side of neck, K26(28:28:30:32)sts from back. [64(68:68:70:78)sts]

Work in K1, P1 rib for 8cm [3¼in].

Using a 5mm needle, cast off loosely in rib.

Join left shoulder and Neck Border, reversing seam for turn back on Neck Border.

Join side and sleeve seams.

Insert sleeves.

Press seams.

Thread ribbons through eyelets and secure on w.s.

6 Lavinia

Heath

Breed: Herdwick
Category: Mountain and Hill

What better than Herdwick for a man's jacket with its textured yoke to bring out the ruggedness of the yarn and the glory of the breed's natural colouring. Either leather or horn buttons can be used.

MATERIALS

Hand Spun – Herdwick
5.5 threads per cm – Single ply
13 threads per in – Single ply

Commercial Equivalent – Chunky
3 threads per cm
7/8 threads per in
625(650:675:700)g of Herdwick.
Pair each 5½mm and 7mm knitting needles.
9 Buttons.
NB If using a commercial yarn allow extra.

MEASUREMENTS

To fit chest 97(102:107:112)cm [38(40:42:44)in].
Length from top of shoulders 66(67:68:69)cm [26(26½:26¾:27¼)in].
Sleeve seam 48(49:49:50)cm [19(19¼:19¼:19¾)in].

TENSION

14 sts and 19 rows to 10cm [4 in] measured over stocking stitch on 7mm needles.
11 sts and 20 rows to 10cm [4in] measured over pattern on 7mm needles.

BACK

With 5½mm needles, cast on 71(75:79:83)sts and work in K1, P1 rib, rows on r.s. having a K1 at each end, for 7cm [2¾in], ending with r.s. facing.
Change to 7mm needles and work in st.st until Back measures 48(49:50:51)cm [19(19¼:19¾:20)in], ending with a P row.

Next row [K2, K2tog] 1(7:13:9) times, [K3, K2tog] 13(9:5:9) times, K2. [57(59:61:65)sts]
K 3 rows.
Cont in patt as folls:
1st row K.
2nd row K1, * [P1, yrn, P1, yrn, P1] in next st, K1; rep from * to end.
3rd row P.
4th row K1, * yft, sl2P, P3tog, p2sso, K1; rep from * to end.
5th row K.
6th row K2, * [P1, yrn, P1, yrn, P1] in next st, K1; rep from * to last st, K1.
7th row P.
8th row K2, * yft, sl2P, P3tog, p2sso, K1; rep from * to last st, K1.
These 8 rows form patt.
Rep 1st–8th rows 3 times more.
Cast off 18(19:19:21)sts at beg of next 2 rows for shoulders.
Leave rem 21(21:23:23)sts on a spare needle.

LEFT FRONT

With 5½mm needles, cast on 35(37:39:41)sts and work in rib as given for Back.
Change to 7mm needles and work in st.st. until Front matches Back to g.st ridges, ending with a P row.
Next row [K2, K2tog] 1(5:3:1) times, [K3, K2tog] 5(3:5:7) times, K2. [29(29:31:33)sts]
K 3 rows.
Working in patt as given for Yoke on Back, for 16(16:14:14) rows, thus ending with r.s. facing.
Keeping patt correct, *shape front neck* as folls:
Next row Patt to last 5(5:6:6)sts, not including any sts made in patt, turn and leave rem 5(5:6:6)sts on a safety pin.
Dec 1 st at neck edge on next and every foll alt row until 18(19:19:21)sts rem.
Work a few rows straight until Front matches Back to shoulder, ending with r.s. facing.
Cast off rem sts.

RIGHT FRONT

Work as for Left Front, reversing shapings.

7 Heath

SLEEVES

With 5½mm needles, cast on 34(34:36:36)sts and work in K1, P1 rib for 6cm [2¼in].

Next row Rib 3(3:4:4), M1 [rib 4, M1] 7 times, rib to end. [42(42:44:44)sts]

Change to 7mm needles and work in st.st. *shaping sides* by inc 1 st at each end of 3rd and every foll 6th(5th:5th:5th) row until there are 64(68:70:70)sts.

Work straight until sleeve measures 48(49:49:50)cm [19(19¼:19¼:19¾)in], ending with a P row.
Cast off.

MAKE UP AND BORDERS

Join shoulder seams.

Neck Border With r.s. facing, 5½mm needles, starting at top of right front, K5(5:6:6)sts from safety-pin, *Knit up* 14(14:16:16)sts to shoulder, K21(21:23:23)sts from back, *Knit up* 14(14:16:16) sts down left side of neck, K5(5:6:6)sts from safety-pin. [59(59:67:67)sts]
Work in P1, K1 rib for 4cm [1½in], rows on w.s. having a P 1 at each end.
Cast off neatly in rib.

Button Border With 5½mm needles, cast on 7 sts.
1st row (R.S.), K2, [P1, K1] twice, K1.
2nd row K1 [P1, K1] 3 times.
Rep these 2 rows until strip, when slightly stretched, fits up Right Front to top of Neck Border.
Sew in position as you go along. Cast off evenly in rib.

Buttonhole Border Work as for Button Border with the addition of 9 buttonholes, first to come 2cm [¾in] above lower edge, last to come at centre of Neck Border and remainder spaced evenly between.
First mark position of buttons on Button Border to ensure even spacing, then work to correspond.
To make a buttonhole (R.S.), rib 2, cast off 2, rib to end and back casting on 2 over those cast off.
Measure down 23(24:25:25)cm [9(9½:9¾:9¾)in] from each shoulder and place markers on Back and Fronts.
Sew Sleeves in between markers. Join side and sleeve seams.
Press seams. Sew on buttons.

Dorothea

Breed: Shetland
Category: Shortwool and Down

Finely combed white Shetland brings out the beauty of the stitch used in this all-over lacey patterned jumper with its attractive ribbed shoulders. It will look just as lovely in any other of the three natural Shetland shades, black, grey or moorit.

MATERIALS

Hand Spun – Shetland
10 threads per cm – Single ply
25 threads per in – Single ply

Commercial Equivalent – Double knitting (thin)
5.5 threads per cm
14 threads per in
225(250:275:300)g of Combed Shetland Wool.
Pair each 3mm and 4mm knitting needles, A 3mm crochet hook.
3 small buttons.
NB If using a commercial yarn allow extra.

MEASUREMENTS

To fit bust 81(86:91–97:102)cm [32(34:36–38:40)in].
Length from top of shoulders 55(56:59:61)cm [21¾(22:23¼:24)in].
Sleeve seam 44cm [17¼in].

TENSION

24 sts and 36 rows to 10cm [4in] measured over pattern on 4mm needles.

BACK

**With 3mm needles, cast on 92(100:108:116)sts and work in K1, P1 rib for 7cm [2¾in].
Next row Rib 7(8:9:7), M1, [rib 13(14:15:17), M1] 6 times, rib to end. [99(107:115:123)sts

Change to 4mm needles and work in patt as folls:
1st row K.
2nd, 4th and 6th rows P.
3rd row K2, * yfwd, K2tog, yfwd, K2togtbl; rep from * to last st, K1.
5th row K.
7th row K3, * K2tog, yfwd, K1, yfwd, sl1 K, K1, psso, K3; rep from * to end.
8th row P2, * P2togtbl, yrn, P3, yrn, P2tog, P1; rep from * to last st, P1.
9th row K1, K2tog, * yfwd, K5, yfwd, sl1 K, K2tog, psso; rep from * to last 8sts, yfwd, K5, yfwd, sl1, K1, psso, K1.
10th row P2, * yrn, P2tog, P3, P2togtbl, yrn, P1; rep from * to last st, P1.
11th row K3, * yfwd, sl1 K, K1, psso, K1, K2tog, yfwd, K3; rep from * to end.
12th row P4, * yrn, sl1 P, P2tog, psso, yrn, P5; rep from * to last 7 sts, yrn, sl1 P, P2tog, psso, yrn, P4.
These 12 rows form patt.
Work straight in patt until Back measures 36cm [14¼in], ending with r.s. facing.
Shape armholes, keeping patt correct, by casting off 3(3:4:4)sts at beg of next 2 rows.
Dec 1 st at each end of next 3(5:5:7) rows, then on every alt row until 77(81:85:89)sts rem.
Work straight until armhole measures 11(12:15:17)cm [4¼(4¾:6:6¾)in], ending with r.s. facing.**
Divide for back opening and work in K1, P1 rib as folls:
Next row Rib 38(40:42:44), turn and leave rem sts on a spare needle.
Cont on these sts for first side and work straight until armhole measures 19(20:23:25)cm [7½(8:9:9¾)in], ending with r.s. facing.
Shape shoulder by casting off 7(7:8:8)sts at beg of next and foll alt row. Work 1 row. Cast off 8(8:7:7)sts, place rem 16(18:19:21)sts on a length of yarn.
With r.s. facing, rejoin yarn to rem sts, cast off centre st, work in K1, P1 rib to end.
Work to match first side, reversing shapings.

FRONT

Work as for Back from ** to **.
Work in K1, P1 rib (rows on r.s. having a K1 at each end) until armhole measures 12(13:16:18)cm

8 Dorothea

[$4\frac{3}{4}$($5\frac{1}{4}$:$6\frac{1}{4}$:7)in], ending with r.s. facing.

Divide for front neck, keeping rib correct, as folls:

Next row Rib 29(30:32:33), K2tog, turn and leave rem sts on a spare needle.

Cont in rib, dec 1 st at neck edge on every row until 22(22:23:23)sts rem.

Work a few rows straight until Front matches Back to shoulder, ending with r.s. facing.

Shape shoulder by casting off 7(7:8:8)sts at beg of next and foll alt row. Work 1 row. Cast off rem 8(8:7:7)sts.

With r.s. facing, slip centre (15(17:17:19)sts on a length of yarn, rejoin yarn to rem sts, K2tog, rib to end.

Work to match first side, reversing shapings.

SLEEVES

With 3mm needles, cast on 52(54:56:58)sts and work in K1, P1 rib for 5cm [2in].

Next row Rib 5(5:3:5), M1 [rib 7(11:5:6), M1] 6(4:10:8) times, rib to end. [59(59:67:67)sts]

Change to 4mm needles and work in patt as given for Back, *shaping sides* by inc 1 st at each end of 7th and every foll 8th row until there are 83(83:91:91)sts, taking inc sts into patt.

Work straight until Sleeve measures approx 44cm [$17\frac{1}{4}$in], ending with same row of patt as on Back and Front.

Shape top, keeping patt correct, by casting off 3(3:4:4)sts at beg of next 2 rows.

2ND, 3RD AND 4TH SIZES
Dec 1 st at each end of next row. Work 3 rows.
Rep last 4 rows 1(2:5) times more.

ALL SIZES
Dec 1 st at each end of next and every foll alt row until 25 sts rem, ending with r.s. facing.
Cast off rem sts.

MAKE UP AND NECK BORDER

Press lightly on wrong side with damp cloth and warm iron.
Join shoulders.

Neck Border With r.s. facing, starting at left back, using 3mm needles, rib 16(18:19:21)sts from back, *Knit up* 23 sts down left side of neck, rib 15(17:17:19)sts from front, *Knit up* 23 sts up right side of neck, rib 16(18:19:21)sts from back. [93(99:101:107)sts]

Work in K1, P1 rib for 2.5cm [1in].

Cast off neatly in rib. Work 1 row of dc around back opening, making 3 loops of 2 ch for buttonholes.

Join side and sleeve seams.
Insert sleeves.
Press seams. Sew on buttons.

3 WOOL BLEND

It is very important when blending fibres on either hand carders or a drum carder to try and complete the blending of the whole amount required, as far as is possible, in one session, unless a very detailed breakdown of the mixture is recorded. Metric certainly helps in this instance.

Wool and Mohair is a lovely combination and white Mohair with Shetland moorit (more red) simply glows.

It is not necessary to use 50% wool/50% Mohair, though perhaps trying to use a wool base is certainly safer for a longer lasting garment. Two-third wool/one-third Mohair is quite sufficient and in some cases three-quarters wool/one-quarter other fibre is enough.

Lay a small amount of wool on the carders followed by a layer of Mohair (or whatever other fibre you wish to blend i.e. dog, cat, angora, cashmere, alpaca) and proceed to card. The yarn will come out evenly blended.

Whilst the blending of your yarn is important so also is the way you use the skeins in knitting. If, for instance, you have used random Jacob and you have a skein which has rather more of the white than the black or grey, then either:

1 break off the yarn at intervals and continue with another shade to even blend.

2 use two balls of yarn at the same time and alternate the balls every second row, thus staggering the colour change,

3 note, perhaps, a large patch of white on one side of the front of a garment and marrying the other front with similar shade changes as far as possible.

This all adds to the ultimate professional finish of garments, as though not only did you plan and design your own yarn, but also you have carried the professionalism through in making the best use of that yarn throughout the making of the garment. The reward is that the garment will be an exclusive only to you. The shape and pattern will be similar but different use of yarns will always create a completely different visual effect to any end product.

Morag

Category: Shortwool and Down
Breed: Shetland
Other Fibres: Goat hair

A glowing combination of Shetland moorit and mohair was used in this very attractive V-necked sweater with saddle shoulders. An interesting feature is the use of lace within the alternate cables.

Note: A very satisfactory combination on all luxury yarns is to use two-thirds wool to one-third of the luxury yarn.

MATERIALS

Hand Spun– Shetland and Mohair (blended $\frac{2}{3}$ to $\frac{1}{3}$)
7 threads per cm – Single ply
17 threads per in – Single ply

Commercial Equivalent – Aran type (thick)
4 threads per cm
10 threads per in

400(425:450;475)g of Wool and Mohair.
Pair each 4mm and 5½mm knitting needles. Cable needle.
NB If using a commercial yarn allow extra.

MEASUREMENTS

To fit bust 81(86:91:97:102)cm [32(34:36:38:40)in].
Length from top of shoulders 59(60;61;62;64)cm [23¼(23½;24;24½;25¼)in].
Sleeve seam 46cm [18in].

TENSION

18 sts and 22 rows to 10cm [4in] measured over stocking stitch on 5½mm needles.

SPECIAL ABBREVIATIONS

Tw2 = Twist 2 by knitting together next 2 sts through back of loops, then before slipping sts off needle, K into back of first stitch again.

C8B = slip next 4 sts onto cable needle and leave at back of work, K4, then K4 from cable needle.
C7F = slip next 2 sts onto cable needle and leave at front of work, Tw2, yfwd, sl1, K2tog, psso, yfwd, then Tw2 from cable needle.

BACK

**With 4mm needles, cast on 74(78:82:88:92)sts and work in K1, P1 rib for 8cm [3¼in].
Next row Rib 2, M1, [rib 4, M1] 3(5:7:21:8) times, [rib 3(3:3:0:5), M1] 14(10:6:0:4) times, [rib 4, M1] 4(6:8:0:9) times, rib 2. [96(100:104:110:114)sts]
Change to 5½mm needles and work in patt as folls:
1st row (R.S.), P4(6:5:8:7), [Tw2, yfwd, sl1, K2tog, psso, yfwd, Tw2, P6(6:7:7:8), K8, P6(6:7:7:8)] 3 times, Tw2, yfwd, sl1, K2tog, psso, yfwd, Tw2, P4(6:5:8:7).
2nd and every alt row K4(6:5:8:7), [P7, K6(6:7:7:8), P8, K6(6:7:7:8)] 3 times, P7, K4(6:5:8:7).
3rd row P4(6:5:8:7), [Tw2, yfwd, sl1, K2tog, psso, yfwd, Tw2, P6(6:7:7:8), C8B, P6(6:7:7:8)] 3 times, Tw2, yfwd, sl1, K2tog, psso, yfwd, Tw2, P4(6:5:8:7).
5th and 7th rows As 1st.
9th row P4(6:5:8:7), [C7F, P6(6:7:7:8), K8, P6(6:7:7:8)] 3 times, C7F, P4(6:5:8:7).
11th row As 1st.
12th row As 2nd.
These 12 rows form patt.
Work straight until Back measures 38cm [15in], ending with r.s. facing.**
Shape armholes, keeping patt correct by casting off 3(4:4:5:5)sts at beg of next 2 rows. Dec 1 st at each end of next 3 rows. Work 1 row.
Dec 1 st at each end of next and every foll alt row until 72(74:78:80:82)sts rem.
Work straight until Back measures 54(55:56:57:59)cm [21¼(21¾:22:22½:23¾)in], ending with r.s. facing.
Shape shoulders by casting off 6(6:7:7:7)sts at beg of next 4 rows, then 6(7:6:7:7)sts at beg of foll 2 rows.
Keeping patt correct, work straight on rem 36(36:38:38:40)sts for a further 5cm [2in], ending with r.s. facing.
Leave sts on a spare needle.

9 Morag

FRONT

Work as for Back from ** to **.

Shape armhole and *divide for neck*, keeping patt correct as folls:

Next row Cast off 3(4:4:5:5)sts, patt 43(44:46: 48:50) [including st on needle after cast off], K2tog, turn and leave rem sts on a spare needle.

Cont in patt on these sts for first side, dec 1 st at neck edge on every alt row *at the same time* dec 1 st at armhole edge on next 3 rows, then on foll 5(6:6:7:8) alt rows. [29(28:30:30:30)sts]

Cont dec at neck edge *only* on every alt row until 18(19:20:21:21)sts rem.

Work a few rows straight until Front matches Back to shoulder, ending with r.s. facing.

Shape shoulder by casting off 6(6:7:7:7)sts at beg of next and foll alt row.

Work 1 row. Cast off rem 6(7:6:7:7)sts.

With r.s. facing, rejoin yarn to rem sts, K2tog, patt to end.

Work to match first side, reversing shapings.

SLEEVES

With 4mm needles, cast on 40(42:42:44:46)sts and work in K1, P1 rib for 7cm [2¾in].

Next row Rib 2, M1, [rib 4, M1] 1(2:2:3:4) times [rib 3, M1] 8(6:6:4:2) times, [rib 4, M1] 2(3:3:4:5) times, rib 2. [52(54:54:56:58)sts]

Change to 5½mm needles and work in patt as folls:

1st row (R.S.), P7(8:8:9:10), Tw2, yfwd, sl1, K2tog, psso, yfwd, Tw2, P6, K8, P6, Tw2, yfwd, sl1, K2tog, psso, yfwd, Tw2, P7(8:8:9:10).

2nd row K7(8:8:9:10), P7, K6, P8, K6, P7, K7(8:8:9:10).

Cont working cables as given for Back, *shaping sides* by inc 1 st at each end of 5th and every foll 6th row until there are 72(76:78:80:82)sts, taking inc sts into reverse st.st.

Work straight until sleeve measures 46cm [18in], ending with r.s. facing.

Shape top, keeping patt correct, by casting off 3(4:4:5:5)sts at beg of next 2 rows.

Dec 1 st at each end of next and every alt row until 42(42:42:38:34)sts rem, ending with r.s. facing.

Dec 1 st at each end of every row until 22 sts rem.

Keeping patt correct, work straight on these 22 sts until strip, when slightly stretched, fits along shoulder edge, ending with r.s. facing.

Left Sleeve Cast off 11 sts, work to end.

Right Sleeve Work 11 sts, cast off rem sts.

Both Sleeves Leave rem 11 sts on a spare needle.

MAKE UP AND NECK BORDER

Do not press.

Join shoulders to saddle strips, leaving left back shoulder open, then join cast-off edge of right saddle strip to extra rows at top of back.

Neck Border With r.s. facing and 4mm needles, starting at centre of left saddle, K11 sts from sleeve, *Knit up* 31(33:35:37:39)sts down left side of neck, pick up loop at centre V and knit into back of it (mark this st), *Knit up* 31(33:35:37:39) sts up right side of neck, K11 sts from right saddle, K36(36:38:38:40)sts from back dec 4 sts evenly. [117(121:127:131:137)sts]

1st row *P1, K1; rep from * to within 2 sts of marked st, P2tog, P1, P2togtbl, ** K1, P1; rep from ** to end.

2nd row K1, * P1, K1; rep from * to within 2 sts of marked st, P2togtbl, K1, P2tog, K1, ** P1, K1; rep from ** to end.

Rep these 2 rows for 3cm [1¼in], ending with 1st row.

Cast off evenly in rib dec as before.

Join left back shoulder to saddle strip, then join cast-off edge of left saddle to extra rows at top of back.

Join Neck Border.

Join side and sleeves seams.

Insert sleeves.

Press seams.

Michael

Breed: Shetland
Category: Shortwool and Down
Other fibre: Goat hair

A complete blend of light grey Shetland wool and light grey Mohair give this soft handling V-necked cabled sweater a unisex appeal.

MATERIALS

Hand Spun – Shetland and Mohair
9 threads per cm – Single ply
22 threads per in – Single ply

Commercial Equivalent – Double Knitting (thick)
5 threads per cm
12 threads per in
425(450:475:525:550:575)g of Wool and Mohair.
Pair each 3¼mm and 4½mm knitting needles. Cable needle.
NB If using a commercial yarn allow extra.

MEASUREMENTS

To fit bust/chest 86(91:97:102:107:112)cm [34(36:38:40:42:44)in].
Length from top of shoulders 61(63:64:66:67:68)cm [24(24¾:25¼:26:26½:26¾)in].
Sleeve seam 46(46:46:47:47:48)cm [18(18:18:18½:18½:19)in].

TENSION

20 sts and 26 rows to 10cm [4in] measured over stocking stitch on 4½mm needles.

SPECIAL ABBREVIATIONS

C6B = slip next 3 sts onto cable needle and leave at back of work, K3, then K3 from cable needle.
C6F = slip next 3 sts onto cable needle and leave at front of work, K3, then K3 from cable needle.

PANEL PATTERN (16 sts)

1st row P2, [C6B] twice, P2.
2nd row K2, P12, K2.
3rd row P2, K3, C6F, K3, P2.
4th row As 2nd.
These 4 rows form panel patt.

BACK

**With 3¼mm needles, cast on 90(96:102:106:112:116)sts and work in K1, P1 rib for 7cm [2¾in].
Next row Rib 2(5:8:2:5:7), M1, [rib 5(5:5:6:6:6), M1] 17 times, rib to end. [108(114:120:124:130:134)sts]
Change to 4½mm needles and work in st.st. placing panels as folls:
1st row K15(18:21:20:23:25), Panel Patt 16 sts as 1st row, K15(15:15:18:18:18) twice, Panel Patt 16 sts as 1st row, K to end.
2nd row P15(18:21:20:23:25), Panel Patt 16 sts as 2nd row, P15(15:15:18:18:18) twice, Panel Patt 16 sts as 2nd row, P to end.
Cont thus working appropriate rows of Panel Patt until Back measures 39cm [15¼in], ending with r.s. facing.
Shape raglans, keeping patt correct, by casting off 5(5:6:6:7:7)sts at beg of next 2 rows. **
3rd row K2, K2tog, patt to last 4 sts, K2togtbl, K2.
4th row P3, patt to last 3 sts, P3.
Rep 3rd and 4th rows until 48(50:48:46:48:46)sts rem, ending with 4th row.

1ST, 2ND, 3RD, 4TH AND 5TH SIZES
Next row K2, K3tog, patt to last 5 sts, K3togtbl, K2.
Next row P3, patt to last 3 sts, P3.
Rep last 2 rows 2(2:1:0:0) times more.

ALL SIZES
Leave rem 36(38:40:42:44:46)sts on a spare needle.

FRONT

Work as for Back from ** to **.
Divide for neck as folls:
3rd row K2, K2tog, patt 43(46:48:50:52:54), K2tog, turn and leave rem sts on a spare needle.

10 Michael

4th row Patt to last 3 sts, P3.
5th row K2, K2tog, patt to last 2 sts, K2tog.
6th row Patt to last 3 sts, P3.
Rep 5th and 6th rows until 37(40:42:44:44:46)sts rem, ending with 6th row.
Next row K2, K2tog, patt to last 2 sts, K2tog.
Next row Patt to last 3 sts, P3.
Next row K2, K2tog, patt to end.
Next row Patt to last 3 sts, P3.
Rep last 4 rows until 10(10:6:5:5:4)sts rem, ending with r.s. facing.

1ST, 2ND, 4TH, 5TH AND 6TH SIZES
Next row K2, K2tog, patt to end.
Next row Patt to last 3 sts, P3.

1ST, 2ND AND 3RD SIZES
Next row K2, K3tog, patt to end.
Next row Patt to last 3 sts, P3.
Rep last 2 rows 1(1:0) time. [4 sts].

1ST, 2ND, 3RD, 4TH AND 5TH SIZES
Next row K1, K3tog.
Next row P2.

6TH SIZE
Next row K1, K2tog.
Next row P2.

ALL SIZES
Next row K2tog and fasten off.
With r.s. facing, rejoin yarn to rem sts, K2tog, patt to last 4 sts, K2togtbl, K2.
Work to match first side, reversing shapings, noting that K2togtbl will be worked in place of K2tog at raglan shapings.

SLEEVES

With 3¼mm needles, cast on 44(46:48:48:50:52) sts and work in K1, P1 rib for 6cm [2¼in].
Next row Rib 2(3:4:1:2:3), M1, [rib 3, M1] 13(13: 13:15:15:15) times, rib to end. [58(60:62:64:66: 68)sts]
Change to 4½mm needles and work in st.st. placing panels as folls:
1st row K3(5:7:6:8:10), Panel Patt 16 sts as 1st row, K20(18:16:20:18:16), Panel Patt 16 sts as 1st row, K3(5:7:6:8:10).
2nd row P3(5:7:6:8:10), Panel Patt as 2nd row, P20(18:16:20:18:16), Panel Patt 16 sts as 2nd row, P3(5:7:6:8:10).
Cont thus working appropriate rows of panel patt, *shaping sides* by inc 1 st each end of 5th and every foll 8th(7th:7th:7th:6th:6th) row until there are 82(86:90:92:96:98)sts, taking inc sts into st.st.
Work straight until sleeve measures 46(46:46:47: 47:48)cm [18(18:18:18½:18½:19)in] ending with r.s. facing.
Shape raglans, keeping patt correct, by casting off 5(5:6:6:7:7)sts at beg of next 2 rows.
3rd row K2, K2tog, patt to last 4 sts, K2togtbl, K2.
4th row P3, patt to last 3 sts, P3.
Rep 3rd and 4th rows until 22(22:18:14:14:10)sts rem, ending with 4th row.

1ST, 2ND, 3RD, 4TH AND 5TH SIZES
Next row K2, K3tog, patt to last 5 sts, K3togtbl, K2.
Next row P3, patt to last 3 sts, P3.
Rep last 2 rows 2(2:1:0:0) times. [10sts]

ALL SIZES
Leave rem 10 sts on a spare needle.

MAKE UP AND NECK BORDER

Join raglans, leaving left back raglan open.

Neck Border With r.s. facing, 3¼mm needles, K10 sts from sleeve, *Knit up* 39(41:43:47:49:51)sts down left side of neck, pick up loop at centre V and Knit into back of it [mark this st] *Knit up* 39(41:43:47:49:51)sts up right side of neck, K10 sts from sleeve, K sts from back working K2tog across top of cable. [129(135:141:151:157:163) sts]
1st row K1, *P1, K1; rep from * to within 2 sts of marked st, P2tog, P1, P2togtbl, **K1, P1; rep from ** to last st, K1.
2nd row *P1, K1; rep from * to within 2 sts of marked st, P2togtbl, K1, P2tog, **K1, P1; rep from ** to end.
Rep these 2 rows for 3cm [1¼in], ending with 1st row.
Cast off evenly in rib, dec as before.
Join rem raglan and Neck Border.
Join side and sleeve seams.
Press seams.

4 PLYED YARNS

The straightforward plying of two different fibres make very interesting yarns.

Try plying one strand of light moorit (Shetland) with one strand of samoyed dog hair! A light brown/red background with a pure white fluffy surface.

The following designs have been created by using the beautiful wool/cultivated silk (bombyx mori) combination and to add a dash to this combination we have on two of the designs added a commercial glitter as a third yarn!

Thane

Breed: Shetland
Category: Shortwool and Down
Other Fibre: Silk

Dress up or down this lace and cabled patterned sweater, the unique yarn of which has been created by using one strand of Shetland wool and one strand of pure silk together with a third strand of a commercial silver/gold glitter yarn – all plyed together.

MATERIALS

Hand Spun – Silk
14 threads per cm – Single ply
35 threads per in – Single ply

Hand Spun – Shetland
10 threads per cm – Single ply
25 threads per in – Single ply

Commercial Glitter Yarn (plyed with Shetland and Silk)

10 threads per cm
25 threads per in

Commercial Equivalent – Chunky

3 threads per cm
7 threads per in
625(700)g of Shetland, Silk and Commercial Glitter.
Approx 8(10) balls of Commercial Glitter is required.
Pair each 4½mm and 6mm knitting needles. Cable needle.
NB If using a commercial yarn allow extra.

MEASUREMENTS

To fit bust 81–86(91–97)cm [32–34(36–38)in].
Length from top of shoulders 60(62)cm [23½ (24½)in].
Sleeve seam 46(47)cm [18(18½)in].

TENSION

19 sts and 24 rows to 10cm [4in] measured over pattern on 6mm needles.

SPECIAL ABBREVIATIONS

C6F = slip next 3 sts onto cable needle and leave at front of work, K3 then K3 from cable needle.

BACK

**With 4½mm needles, cast on 74(84)sts and work in K1, P1 rib for 6cm [2¼in].

Next row Rib 4(9), M1, [rib 6, M1] 11(12) times, rib to end. [86(97)sts]

Change to 6mm needles and work in patt as folls:

1st row K2, * yfwd, sl1, K1, psso, K1, K2tog, yfwd, K6; rep from * to last 7 sts, yfwd, sl1, K1, psso, K1, K2tog, yfwd, K2.

2nd and every alt row P.

3rd row K3, * yfwd, sl1, K2tog, psso, yfwd, K1, C6F, K1; rep from * to last 6 sts, yfwd, sl1, K2tog, psso, yfwd, K3.

5th row As 1st.

7th row K3, * yfwd, sl1, K2tog, psso, yfwd, K8; rep from * to last 6 sts, yfwd, sl1, K2tog, psso, yfwd, K3.

8th row As 2nd.

These 8 rows form patt.**

Work straight until Back measures 60(62)cm [23½(24½)in], ending with r.s. facing.

Shape shoulders by casting off 28(32)sts at beg of next 2 rows.

Leave rem 30(33)sts on a spare needle.

FRONT

Work as for Back from ** to **.

Work straight until Front matches Back to shoulder less 18 rows.

Divide for neck, keeping patt correct, as folls:

Next row Patt 34(37), K2tog, turn and leave rem sts on a spare needle.

Cont on these sts for first side, dec 1 st at neck edge on every row until 28(32)sts rem.

Work a few rows straight until Front matches Back to shoulder, ending with r.s. facing. Cast off rem sts.

With r.s. facing, slip centre 14(15)sts on a spare needle, rejoin yarn to rem sts, K2tog, patt to end.

Work to match first side, reversing shapings.

SLEEVES (both sizes the same)

With 4½mm needles, cast on 40 sts and work in K1, P1 rib for 5cm [2in].

Next row Rib 2, M1, [rib 3, M1] 12 times, rib 2. [53sts].

Change to 6mm needles and work in patt as given for Back, *shaping sides* by inc 1 st at each end of 5th and every foll 8th row until there are 75 sts, taking inc sts into patt.

Work straight until sleeve measures 46(47)cm [18(18½)in], ending with r.s. facing. Cast off.

MAKE UP AND NECK BORDER

Join right shoulder seam.

Neck border With r.s. facing, 4½mm needles, *Knit up* 14 sts down left side of neck, K across 14(15)sts from front dec 2 sts evenly, *Knit up* 14 sts up right side of neck, K30(33)sts from back dec 4 sts evenly. [66(70)sts].

Work in K1, P1 rib for 7cm [2¾in].

Using a 6mm needle, cast off loosely in rib.

Join left shoulder and Neck Border.

Fold Neck Border in half to wrong side and slip hem loosely in position.

Measure down 21cm [8¼in] from shoulders on Front and Back, placing markers.

Place centre of cast-off edge of sleeve to shoulder and sew in position between markers.

Join side and sleeve seams.

Press seams.

Elizabeth

Breed: Shetland
Category: Shortwool and Down
Other Fibre: Silk

The main feature of this beautiful cardigan is the beaded smocking on the yoke and welts, although the beading is optional. The one strand of wool and one strand of cultivated silk is a lovely combination and we have as a final touch used hand-carved horn buttons.

MATERIALS

Hand Spun – Shetland
9 threads per cm – Single ply
22 threads per in – Single ply

Hand Spun – Silk
14 threads per cm – Single ply
35 threads per in – Single ply

Commercial Equivalent – Double Knitting (thick)
5 threads per cm
12 threads per in

450(475:500:525)g of Shetland and Silk.
Pair each 3mm and 4mm knitting needles.
Approx 500 small beads. 7 Buttons.
NB If using a commercial yarn allow extra.

MEASUREMENTS

To fit bust 81(86:91:97)cm [32(34:36:38)in].
Length from top of shoulders 55(56:57:58)cm [21¼(22:22½:22¾)in].
Sleeve seam 44cm [17¼in].

TENSION

27 sts and 30 rows to 10cm [4in] measured over P2, K1 rib on 4mm needles.

BACK

With 3mm needles, cast on 147(155:163:171)sts and K3 rows.
Work in rib as folls:
1st row P3, * K1, P3; rep from * to end.
2nd row K3, * P1, K3; rep from * to end.
Rep 1st and 2nd rows 12 times more.
Place markers at each end of last row.
Next row P1, P2tog, * K1, P1, P2tog; rep from * to end. [110(116:122:128)sts]
Change to 4mm needles and cont in K2, P1 rib as set until work measures 34cm [13¼in], ending with r.s. facing.
Shape armholes by casting off 5(5:5:6)sts at beg of next 2 rows.
Dec 1 st at each end of next 3 rows, then on every alt row until 86(92:92:98)sts rem.
Work straight until armhole measures 7(8:9:10)cm, [2¾(3¼:3½:4)in], ending with w.s. facing.
Next row K1, M1, K1, * P1, K1, M1, K1; rep from * to end. [115(123:123:131)sts]
Place markers at each end of last row.
Work in P3, K1 rib as set for 42 rows, thus ending with r.s. facing.
Shape shoulders by casting off 11(12:12:13)sts at beg on next 4 rows, then 12 sts at beg of foll 2 rows.
Leave rem 47(51:51:55)sts on a length of yarn.

LEFT FRONT

With 3mm needles, cast on 75(79:83:87)sts and K 3 rows.
Work 26 rows in rib as given for Back. Place markers at each end of last row.
Next row P1, P2tog, * K1, P1, P2tog; rep from * to end. [56(59:62:65)sts]
Change to 4mm needles and cont in rib as set until Front matches Back to armhole, ending with r.s. facing.
Shape armhole by casting off 5(5:5:6)sts at beg of next row. Work 1 row.
Dec 1 st at armhole edge on next 3 rows, then on every alt row until 44(47:50:50)sts rem.
Work straight until armhole measures 7(8:9:10)cm [2¾(3¼:3½:4)in], ending with w.s. facing.
Next row K1, M1, K1, * P1, K1, M1, K1; rep from * to end. [59(63:67:67)sts]

Jamesina, a simple drop-shoulder, slash-necked sweater made from the very popular Jacob's yarn.

Guinevere, a lace-panelled wedding dress

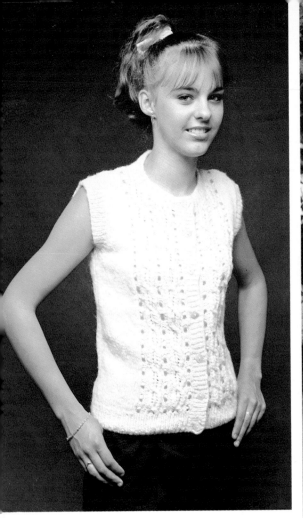

Cheryl, a ribbon-threaded waistcoat

Kirsty, a lace and ribboned sweater

Joseph and Sarah, two children's jumpers

Rosetta, a striped waistcoat

Louise, a silky jumper

Petula, a knitted coat

Morwenna, a drop-shoulder, slash-necked sweater

Ivy, a bomber jacket

Alexandra, a Fair Isle and lace jumper

12 Elizabeth

Place markers at each end of last row.

Work in P3, K1 rib for 21 rows.

Shape neck by casting off 12 sts at beg of next row.

Dec 1 st at neck edge on every row until 34(36:36:38)sts rem.

Work a few rows straight until Front matches Back to shoulder, ending with r.s. facing.

Shape shoulder by casting off 11(12:12:13)sts at beg of next and foll alt row. Work 1 row. Cast off rem 12 sts.

RIGHT FRONT

Work as for Left Front, reversing shapings.

SLEEVES

With 3mm needles, cast on 75(75:79:79)sts and K 3 rows.

Work 16 rows in rib as given for Back.

Next row P1, P2tog, * K1, P1, P2tog; rep from * to end. [56(56:59:59)sts]

Change to 4mm needles and cont in rib as set, *shaping sides* by inc 1 st at each end of 3rd and every foll 6th row until there are 92(92:99:99)sts, taking inc sts into rib.

Work straight until sleeve seam measures 44cm [17¼in], ending with r.s. facing.

Shape top, keeping rib correct, by casting off 5(5:5:6)sts at beg of next 2 rows.

Dec 1 st at each end of next and every alt row until 44(36:44:32)sts rem, ending with r.s. facing.

Dec 1 st at each end of every row until 28(28:29:29)sts rem.

Cast off.

MAKE UP AND BORDERS

Do not press.

Join shoulder seams.

Neck Border With r.s. facing, 3mm needles, *Knit up* 30 sts up right side of neck to shoulder, K47(51:51:55)sts from back, *Knit up* 30 sts down left side of neck. [87(91:91:95)sts]

Work in P1, K1 rib, rows on w.s. having a P1 at each end, for 6cm [2¼in], ending with r.s. facing.

Cast off in rib.

Fold Neck Border in half to w.s. and slip-hem loosely in position.

Buttonhole Border With r.s. facing and 3mm needles, *Knit up* 105(105:111:111)sts from lower edge to top of Neck Border.

1st row K1, * P1, K1; rep from * to end.

2nd row K2, * P1, K1; rep from * to last st, K1.

Rep 1st row once more.

Next row (Buttonhole row), rib 4, * cast off 2 sts, rib 14(14:15:15) including st on needle after cast off; rep from * to last 5 sts, cast off 2, rib to end.

Next row Rib, casting on 2 sts over those cast off.

Work 4 more rows in rib as set.

Cast off neatly in rib.

Button Border With r.s. facing, 3mm needles, starting at top of Neck Border, *Knit up* 105(105:111:111)sts down left front to lower edge.

Work 9 rows in rib as given for Buttonhole Border.

Cast off neatly in rib.

Join side seams.

Smocking Worked over P3, K1 section of garment as folls:

1st row Insert needle through 1st and 2nd rib sts and draw together and stitch in position, sewing a bead on with the last st.

Now draw 3rd and 4th rib sts together and continue in this way across the whole row.

Miss 4 rows.

2nd row Draw 2nd and 3rd rib sts together and cont in this way across whole row.

Miss 4 rows.

Cont working as given until lower edge of garment, sleeve cuffs and yoke have been worked in this way.

Join sleeve seams.

Insert sleeves.

Press seams.

Sew on buttons.

Helen

Breed: Shetland
Category: Shortwool and Down
Other Fibres: Silk

An attractive triangular shaped shawl which has been worked in one strand of wool, one strand cultivated silk and one strand of a commercial silver/gold glitter yarn, plyed together.

MATERIALS

Hand Spun – Silk
14 threads per cm – Single ply
35 threads per in – Single ply

Hand Spun – Shetland
10 threads per cm – Single ply
25 threads per in – Single ply

Commercial Glitter Yarn (plyed with Shetland and Silk)
10 threads per cm
25 threads per in

Commercial Equivalent – Chunky
3 threads per cm
7 threads per in

325g of Shetland, Silk and Commercial Glitter Yarn (approx 4 balls of yarn).
Pair 7mm knitting needles.
No. 6.00mm crochet hook.
NB If using commercial yarn allow extra.

MEASUREMENTS
Depth at centre back approx 86cm [34in].

1st Piece
Cast on 161 sts and work 3 rows in g.st.
Work in *patt* and *shape* as folls:
1st row K6, K2togtbl, K1, * K2tog, K5, yfwd, K1, yfwd, K5, K2togtbl, K1; rep from * to last 8 sts, K2tog, K6.
2nd row P2tog, P to last 2 sts, P2tog.
3rd row K4, K2togtbl, K1, *K2tog, K5, yfwd, K1, yfwd, K5, K2togtbl, K1; rep from * to last 6 sts, K2tog, K4.
4th row P.
5th row K3, K2togtbl, K1, * K2tog, K5, yfwd, K1, yfwd, K5, K2togtbl, K1; rep from * to last 5 sts, K2tog, K3.
6th row As 2nd.
7th row K1, K2togtbl, K1, * K2tog, K5, yfwd, K1, yfwd, K5, K2togtbl, K1; rep from * to last 3 sts, K2tog, K1.
8th row As 4th.
9th row K2togtbl, K1, * K2tog, K5, yfwd, K1, yfwd, K5, K2togtbl, K1; rep from * to last 2 sts, K2tog.
10th row As 2nd.
11th row K3tog, * K5, yfwd, K1, yfwd, K5, K2togtbl, K1, K2tog; rep from * to last 14 sts, K5, yfwd, K1, yfwd, K1, yfwd, K5, sl1, K2tog, psso.
12th row As 4th.
13th row K3tog, K4, * yfwd, K1, yfwd, K5, K2togtbl, K1, K2tog, K5; rep from * to last 8 sts, yfwd, K1, yfwd, K4, sl1, K2tog, psso.
14th row As 2nd.
15th row K3tog, K2, * yfwd, K1, yfwd, K5, K2togtbl, K1, K2tog, K5; rep from * to last 6 sts, yfwd, K1, yfwd, K2, sl1, K2tog, psso.
16th row As 4th.
17th row K2tog, K to last 2 sts, K2tog.
18th row As 17th.
19th row As 2nd.
20th row As 17th. [129 sts.]
Rep last 20 rows 3 times more. [33 sts.]
Work 1st–10th rows again. [17 sts.]
Next row K3tog, K5, yfwd, K1, yfwd, K5, sl1, K2tog, psso.
Next row P.
Next row K3tog, K4, yfwd, K1, yfwd, K4, sl1, K2tog, psso.
Next row P2tog, P to last 2 sts, P2tog.
Next row K3tog, K2, yfwd, K1, yfwd, K2, sl1, K2tog, psso.
Next row P.
Work 17th, 18th and 19th rows again.
Next row K3tog and fasten off.
Work a 2nd piece as given for 1st piece.

MAKE UP

Join pieces to form 1 large triangle.
With r.s. facing, 6.00mm crochet hook, work 1
 row of dc loosely along top edge of triangle.
Fasten off.

Isobel

Breed: Shetland
Category: Shortwool and Down
Other Fibre: Silk

A charmingly feminine jumper in an all-over lace and cable pattern. The cables have been enhanced by threading a narrow satin ribbon in cream through them. The final touch to the jumper being the added frill to the V-shaped neckline.

The yarn is one strand of wool, one strand of silk, plyed together.

MATERIALS

Hand Spun – Shetland
9 threads per cm – Single ply
22 threads per in – Single ply

Hand Spun – Silk
14 threads per cm – Single ply
35 threads per in – Single ply

Commercial Equivalent – Double Knitting (thick)
5 threads per cm
12 threads per in

450(500)g of Shetland and Silk.
Pair each 3¾mm and 4½mm knitting needles.
Circular 4½mm needle. Cable needle.
Approx 8 metres of narrow ribbon, depending on the number of cables threaded.
NB If using a commercial yarn allow extra.

MEASUREMENTS

To fit bust 81–86(91–97)cm [32–34(36–38)in].
Length from top of shoulders 58(60)cm [22¾(23½)in].
Sleeve seam 46cm [18in].

TENSION

24 sts and 30 rows to 10cm [4in] measured over pattern on 4½mm needles.

SPECIAL ABBREVIATIONS

C6 = slip next 3 sts onto cable needle and leave at front of work, K3, then K3 from cable needle.

BACK

**With 3¾mm needles, cast on 96(106)sts and work in K1, P1 rib for 6cm [2¼in].
Next row Rib 3, M1, [rib 9, M1] 10(11) times, rib 3(4). [107(118)sts]
Change to 4½mm needles and work in patt as folls:
1st row K7, * yfwd, sl1, K1, psso, K1, K2tog, yfwd, K6; rep from * to last st, K1.
2nd and every alt row P.
3rd row K1, C6, * K1, yfwd, sl1, K2tog, psso, yfwd, K1, C6; rep from * to last st, K1.
5th row As 1st.
7th row K7, * K1, yfwd, sl1, K2tog, psso, yfwd, K7; rep from * to last st, K1.
8th row As 2nd.
These 8 rows form patt.
Work straight until Back measures 37cm [14½in], ending with r.s. facing.
Shape armholes, keeping patt correct, by casting off 4 sts at beg of next 2 rows.
Dec 1 st at each end of next 5 rows. Work 1 row.**
Dec 1 st at each end of next and every alt row until 75(84)sts rem.
Work straight until armhole measures 21(23)cm [8¼(9)in], ending with r.s. facing.
Shape shoulders by casting off 7(8)sts at beg of next 4 rows, then 6(7)sts at beg of foll 2 rows.
Leave rem 35(38)sts on a spare needle.

FRONT

Work as for Back from ** to **.
Keeping patt correct, cont *shaping armhole* and *divide for neck* as folls:
Next row K2tog, patt 40(46), K2tog, turn and leave rem sts on a spare needle. Cont on these sts for first side, dec 1 st at armhole on every alt row *at the same time* dec 1 st at neck edge on every 3rd row from previous dec until 32(36)sts rem.
Cont dec 1 st at neck edge *only* as before until 20(23)sts rem.
Work a few rows straight until Front matches Back to shoulder, ending with r.s. facing.

14 Isobel

Shape shoulder by casting off 7(8)sts at beg of next and foll alt row. Work 1 row. Cast off rem 6(7)sts.

1ST SIZE
With r.s. facing, slip centre st onto a safety-pin, rejoin yarn to rem sts, K2tog, patt to last 2 sts, K2tog.

2ND SIZE
With r.s. facing, rejoin yarn to rem sts, K2tog, patt to 1st 2 sts, K2tog.

BOTH SIZES
Work to match first side, reversing shapings.

SLEEVES

With 3¾mm needles, cast on 44(48)sts and work in K1, P1 rib for 6 rows.

Shape sides by inc 1 st at each end of next and every foll 8th row until there are 54(58)sts, taking inc sts into rib.

Work straight until rib measures 14cm [5½in], ending with w.s. facing.

Next row Rib 1, M1, [rib 1(3), M1] 4(2) times [rib 2, M1] 22(19) times, [rib 1(3), M1] 4(2) times, rib 1. [85 sts]

Change to 4½mm needles and work in patt as given for Back, until sleeve measures 46cm [18in], ending with same row of patt as on Back and Front.

Shape top, keeping patt correct, by casting off 4 sts at beg of next 2 rows.

Dec 1 st at each end of next and every foll 4th row until 67(61)sts rem. Work 3 rows.

Dec 1 st at each end of next and every alt row until 25 sts rem, ending with r.s. facing.

Cast off.

MAKE UP AND COLLAR

Do not press.

Join right shoulder seam.

1ST SIZE
With circular 4½mm needle, w.s. facing, P35 sts from back dec 3 sts evenly, *Knit up* 40 sts down right side of neck, Kst from safety-pin, *Knit up* 40 sts up left side of neck. [113sts].

2ND SIZE
With circular 4½mm needle, w.s. facing, P38 sts from back inc 1 st at centre, *Knit up* 47 sts down right side of neck, pick up and K loop at centre V, *Knit up* 47 sts up left side of neck. [134 sts]

BOTH SIZES
1st row K5, * P1, K6; rep from * to last 3 sts, P1, K2.

2nd row P2, * M1, K1, M1, P6; rep from * to last 6 sts, M1, K1, M1, P5.

3rd row K5, * P3, K6; rep from * to last 5 sts, P3, K2.

4th row P2, * M1, K3, M1, P6; rep from * to last 8 sts, M1, K3, M1, P5.

5th row K5, * P5, K6; rep from * to last 7 sts, P5, K2.

6th row P2, * M1, K5, M1, P6; rep from * to last 10 sts, M1, K5, M1, P5.

7th row K5, * P7, K6; rep from * to last 9 sts, P7, K2.

8th row P2, * M1, K7, M1, P6; rep from * to last 12 sts, M1, K7, M1, P5.

9th row K5, * P9, K6; rep from * to last 11 sts, P9, K2.

10th row P2, * M1, K9, M1, P6; rep from * to last 14 sts, M1, K9, M1, P5.

11th row K5, * P11, K6; rep from * to last 13 sts, P11, K2.

12th row P2, * K11, P6; rep from * to last 16 sts, K11, P5.

Rep last 2 rows until Collar measures 6cm [2¼in], ending with r.s. facing.

Cast off in rib.

Join left shoulder and Collar, reversing seam on collar.

Join side and sleeve seams.

Insert sleeves.

Using a crochet hook, thread ribbon through cables and secure on w.s. of garment.

5 PLYED SILK

Pure silk has a tendency to stretch and unless used in weaving **must** always be plyed. A very good combination of the use of silk is to use silk waste, which is pure white and when spun gives a towelling effect and Tussah Silk which is a wild silk and is usually a buttery yellow colour. Plyed together they make a very unusual yarn.

Silk comes over from China as fine threads and these threads are what is termed as 'silk thrown', which is a process of twisting and folding the fine threads on themselves to build up a yarn suitable for weaving or knitting. It is during this 'throwing' that the threads sometimes get tangled and have to be cut out. By sorting and cutting this silk waste to reasonably short lengths of 3 to 5in; roughly carded into rolags and fed quite freely onto the spinning wheel you get a yarn with a wonderful towelling effect.

Silk can be quite successfully dyed if kept in a small container during the dyeing process so as not to allow it to move around too much and possibly tangle. It takes commercial dyes very well.

Sabina (skirt and jacket)

Breed: Silk

By plying the richness of Tussah Silk with Silk Waste this delightfully versatile two-piece suit has an unusual towelling effect.

Caroline (camisole)

Worn on its own with a pretty skirt, or casual trousers or teamed with 'Sabrina', the silk suit, makes the very popular camisole a 'must' for the wardrobe.

MATERIALS

Hand Spun

TUSSAH
8 threads per cm – Single ply
20 threads per in – Single ply

SILK WASTE
6 threads per cm – Single ply
15 threads per in – Single ply

Commercial Equivalent – Double-Double
3.5 threads per cm
9.0 threads per in

Jacket   400(450:500:550)g of Silk.

15 Sabrina

Camisole   140(150:160:170)g of Silk.

Skirt   550(600:650:700)g of Silk.

Pair each 4mm, 4½mm, 5mm and 5½mm knitting
  needles.

No. 4½mm crochet hook.

6 Pearl Buttons for Jacket.

4 Pearl Buttons for Camisole.

3 metres of narrow ribbon.

2.5(2.8:3:3.3) metres of lace for edgings.

1 metre of ribbon for shoulder straps.

Length of elastic for Skirt.

NB If using a commercial yarn allow extra.

MEASUREMENTS

Jacket

To fit bust 81(86:91:97)cm [32(34:36:38)in].

Length from top of shoulders 54(55:56:57)cm
  [21¼(21¾:22:22½)in].

Sleeve seam 15cm [6in].

Camisole

To fit bust 81(86:91:97)cm [32(34:36:38)in].

Length 30cm [11¾in].

Skirt

To fit hips 86(91:97:102)cm [34(36:38:40)in].

Length approx 69cm [27¼in] adjustable.

TENSION

18 sts and 24 rows to 10cm [4in] measured over
  stocking stitch on 5mm needles.

17 sts and 22 rows to 10cm [4in] measured over
  stocking stitch on 5½mm needles.

JACKET

BACK

With 4½mm needles, cast on 71(75:79:85)sts and K
  5 rows.

Change to 5½mm needles and work in st.st. until
  Back measures 33cm [13in], ending with a P row.

Shape armholes by casting off 3 sts at beg of next 2
  rows.

Dec 1 st at each end of next 3(3:5:5) rows, then on

every alt row until 55(57:59:61) sts rem.

Work straight until armhole measures 21(22:23:
  24)cm [8¼(8¾:9:9½)in], ending with r.s. facing.

Shape shoulders by casting off 5 sts at beg of next 4
  rows, then 6 sts at beg of foll 2 rows.

Cast off rem 23(25:27:29)sts.

LEFT FRONT

With 4½mm needles, cast on 35(37:39:42)sts and K
  5 rows.

Change to 5½mm needles and work as folls:

1st row K.

2nd row K2, P to end.

Rep last 2 rows until Front matches Back to
  armhole, ending with r.s. facing.

Shape armhole by casting off 3 sts at beg of next
  row. Work 1 row.

Dec 1 st at armhole edge on next 3(3:5:5) rows
  then on every alt row until 27(28:29:30)sts rem.

Work straight until armhole measures 14(15:16:
  17)cm [5½(6:6¼:6¾)in], ending with w.s. facing.

Shape neck by casting off 7 sts at beg of next row.
  Dec 1 st at neck edge on every row until 16 sts
  rem.

Work straight until Front matches Back to
  shoulder, ending with r.s. facing.

Shape shoulder by casting off 5 sts at beg of next
  and foll alt row.

Work 1 row. Cast off rem 6 sts.

RIGHT FRONT

With 4½mm needles, cast on 35(37:39:42)sts and K
  5 rows.

Change to 5½mm needles and work as folls:

1st row K.

2nd row P to last 2 sts, K2.

Work as for Left Front, reversing shapings.

SLEEVES

With 4½mm needles, cast on 49(51:53:55)sts and K
  5 rows.

Change to 5½mm needles and work in st.st.
  shaping sides by inc 1 st at each end of 3rd and
  every foll 4th row until there are 57(59:61:73)sts.

16 Caroline

Work straight until sleeve measures 15cm [6in], ending with a P row.

Shape top by casting off 3 sts at beg of next 2 rows.

Dec 1 st at each end of next and every foll alt row until 17 sts rem, ending with r.s. facing.

Cast off rem sts.

MAKE UP, COLLAR AND BORDERS

Join shoulders.

Collar

With 4½mm needles, starting at inside of cast-off sts on right front, *Knit up* 14 sts to shoulder, K23(25:27:29)sts from back, *Knit up* 14 sts down left side of neck to cast-off sts. [51(53:55:57)sts]

Next row P.

Next row K2, * M1, K2; rep from * to last 3 sts, K3. [75(78:81:84)sts]

Next row K2, P to last 2 sts, K2.

Next row K.

Rep last 2 rows for 3½cm [1½in], ending with a K row. K 5 rows. Cast off.

Join side and sleeve seams.

Insert sleeves.

With No 4½mm crochet hook, work a row of dc down Left Front edge.

Mark position of buttons of Left Front.

Work 1 row of dc up Right Front edge working a loop of 2ch for buttons.

Sew on buttons.

Camisole

With 5½mm needles, cast on 129(137:147:155)sts and P 1 row.

Next row K2, * yfwd, K2tog; rep from * to last st, K1.

Starting with a P row, work in st.st. until garment measures 29cm [11½in], ending with a P row.

Next row K2, * yfwd, K2tog; rep from * to last st, K1.

P 1 row. Cast off.

MAKE UP

Join side seam.

With narrow ribbon, thread through lace edging and camisole, beginning and ending at centre front and tying with a bow to finish.

Sew on shoulder straps, adjusting to fit.

Sew buttons down centre front.

Skirt

BACK AND FRONT (ALIKE)

With 4mm needles, cast on 78(82:88:92)sts and work in K1, P1 rib for 10 rows.

Change to 5mm needles and starting with a K row, work in st.st. for 4 rows.

Shape hips as folls:

Next row K20, M1, K1, M1, K to last 21 sts, M1, K1, M1, K20.

Work 7 rows.

Rep last 8 rows until there are 118(122:128:132)sts.

Work straight until skirt measures 67cm (adjust length, if necessary, here), excluding waist ribbing, ending with a P row.

Change to 4mm needles and work 7 rows in g.st.

Cast off.

MAKE UP

Join side seams.

Cut elastic to fit waist and join in a ring.

Sew to inside of waist ribbing, using a herringbone stitch over elastic to form casing.

Press seams.

6 USE OF COMMERCIAL DYED YARNS

Without going into the wonderful world of natural dyeing as there are many excellent books on the market covering the subject this chapter will deal with adding colour to our hand spun garments. What we have done is to give you three different ways of doing this and then leave it to you to go on . . . and on . . . and on.

Colour Blending

The following eight patterns show you how to add colour to hand spun garments without the necessity of dyeing the yarn yourself.

The colours used were in the form of commercially dyed 'tops'. When purchasing coloured tops (for pastel shades 100g a time of each colour is quite sufficient for several garments) go for the brightest of colours as even the most garish of colours will blend down to lovely pastel shades.

1 It is important to obtain your initial colour first. For example, if you want a very pale lilac, first blend together your blue and red for a deep mauve and by adding a little of the mauve to white you will acquire the palest of lilac.

2 Another important point is blended yarns will, when washed, come up darker, so if a pastel shade is required aim for just an allusion of colour blend on the carders. If the pastel shade is just right at the blending stage, it will inevitably be too dark when washed.

3 Recording. As you make your blended rolag, break off a small piece and stick it into your portfolio, writing the combination alongside, giving you a visual recording of colour for future garments.

Basic shades to have are blue, green, red, yellow and tan. You will already have natural white, grey, brown and black!

Dulcie

Coloured worsted and woollen tops

This bold, long-sleeved sweater was created with commercially dyed yarns to enable the spinner to handle colours without the necessity of dyeing the yarn herself.

MATERIALS

Hand Spun – Worsted and Woollen tops
9 threads per cm – Single ply
22 threads per in – Single ply

Commercial Equivalent – Double Knitting (thick)
5 threads per cm
12 threads per in

Of Dutch Wool 45(50:50:55)g of Main Shade, 200(225:250:275)g of 1st Contrast, 200(225:250: 275)g of 2nd Contrast and 50(55:60:65)g of 3rd Contrast.
Pair each 3¾mm and 4mm knitting needles.
NB If using a commercial yarn allow extra.

MEASUREMENTS

To fit chest/bust 71(76:81:86)cm [28(30:32:34)in]. Length from top of shoulders approx 52(54:54: 55)cm [20½(21¼:21¼:21¾)in]. Sleeve seam approx 39(43:46:46)cm [15¼(17:18: 18)in].

TENSION

21 sts and 30 rows to 10cm [4in] square measured over stocking stitch on 4mm needles.

NOTE

When working pattern as set do not carry yarn across wrong side of work, but use separate balls as required, twisting yarns when changing colour to avoid a hole.

SPECIAL ABBRREVIATIONS

MS = Main Shade; A = 1st Contrast; B = 2nd Contrast; C = 3rd Contrast.

BACK

**With 3¾mm needles and MS, cast on 72(78:84: 88)sts and work in K1, P1 rib for 4(6:6:7)cm [1½(2¼:2¼:2¾)in].
Next row Rib 6(6:6:8), M1, [rib 10(11:12:12), M1] 6 times, rib to end. [79(85:91:95)sts] Break MS.
Change to 4mm needles and joining in colours, work as folls.
1st row K39(42:45:47)A, K1C, K39(42:45:47)B.
2nd row P38(41:44:46)B, P3C, P38(41:44:46)A.
3rd row K37(40:43:45)A, K5C, K37(40:43:45)B.
4th row P36(39:42:44)B, P7C, P36(39:42:44)A.
Cont thus working taking 2 sts more into centre diamond (1 st either side) until 35 sts have been worked in C. Work 1 row.
Now work 2 sts less on every row in C until only 1 st is worked in C, thus ending with right side facing.**
Work 3 more diamonds as given. Work measures approx 52(54:54:55)cm [20½(21¼:21¼:21¾)in].
Shape shoulders by casting off 24(27:29:30)sts at beg of next 2 rows.
Leave rem 31(31:33:35)sts on a spare needle.

FRONT

Work as for Back from ** to **.
Work straight as given for Back until Front matches Back to shoulder less 22(22:24:24) rows.
Divide for neck, keeping patt correct, as folls:
Next row Patt 30(33:35:36)sts, K2tog, turn and leave rem sts on a spare needle.
Dec 1 st at neck edge on every row until 24(27: 29:30)sts rem.
Work a few rows straight until Front matches Back to shoulder, ending with r.s. facing.
Cast off rem sts.
With r.s. facing, slip centre 15(15:17:17)sts on a spare needle, rejoin appropriate colour to rem sts, K2tog, patt to end.
Work to match first side, reversing shapings.

17 Dulcie

SLEEVES

With 3¾mm needles and MS, cast on 38(40:42:44)sts and work in K1, P1 rib for 3(7:4:4)cm [1¼(2¾:1½:1½)in].

Next row Rib 3(3:3:2), M1, [rib 1, M1] 32(34:36:40) times, rib to end. [71(75:79:85)sts] Break MS.

Change to 4mm needles and joining in colours, work as folls:

1ST AND 2ND SIZES

1st row K35(37)A, K1C, K35(37)B.

2nd row P34(36)B, P3C, P34(36)A.

Cont thus working until 3 diamonds have been worked.

Sleeve measures approx 39(43)cm [15¼(17)in]. Cast off.

3RD AND 4TH SIZES

1st row K22(25)A, K35C, K22(25)B.

2nd row P23(26)B, P33C, P23(26)A.

Cont thus working until 3½ diamonds have been worked.

Sleeve measures approx 46cm [18in]. Cast off.

MAKE UP AND NECK BORDER

Join right shoulder.

Neck Border

With r.s. facing, 3¾mm needles and MS, *Knit up* 18(18:20:20)sts down left side of neck, K15(15:17:17)sts from front, *Knit up* 18(18:20:20)sts up right side of neck, K31(31:33:35)sts from back. [82(82:90:92)sts]

Work in K1, P1 rib for 8cm [3¼in].

Using a 4mm needle, cast off loosely in rib.

Join left shoulder and Neck Border.

Fold Neck Border in half to wrong side and slip hem loosely in position.

Measure down 17(18:19:20)cm [6¾(7:7½:8)in] on Back and Front from shoulder.

Place markers, sew in sleeves between markers.

Join side and sleeve seams.

Press seams.

Joseph

Breed: Romney
Category: Longwool and Lustre

An attractive and versatile jumper suitable for children of all ages using the hard-wearing but soft Longwool and Lustre category yarn together with dyed worsted tops for a fun stripe and spot pattern.

MATERIALS

Hand Spun – Romney and Worsted Tops
7 threads per cm – Single ply
17 threads per in – Single ply

Commercial Equivalent – Aran type (thick)
4 threads per cm
10 threads per in

250(275:300:325:350)g of Main Shade, 30(40:50: 60:70)g of 1st Contrast and 20(30:40:50:60)g of 2nd Contrast.
Pair each 4mm and 5mm knitting needles.
NB If using a commercial yarn allow extra.

MEASUREMENTS

To fit chest 51(56:61:66:71)cm [20(22:24:26: 28)in].
Length from top of shoulders 34(39:43:47:50)cm [13½(15¼:17:18½:19¾)in].
Sleeve seam 25(27:31:35:39)cm [9¾(10½:12¼:13¾: 15¼)in].

TENSION

18 sts and 28 rows to 10cm [4in] measured over pattern on 5mm needles.

SPECIAL ABBREVIATIONS

MS = Main Shade; 1st C = 1st Contrast; 2nd = 2nd Contrast.

BACK

**With 4mm needles and MS, cast on 44(48:54: 58:62)sts and work in K1, P1 rib for 3(3:4:4:4)cm [1¼(1¼:1¼:1½:1½)in].
Next row Rib 4(4:5:7:7), M1, [rib 9(10:11:11: 12), M1] 4 times, rib 4(4:5:7:7). [49(53:59:63: 67)sts]
Change to 5mm needles and work in patt as folls:
1st, 3rd, 5th, 7th and 9th rows In MS, K.
2nd, 4th, 6th, 8th and 10th rows In MS, P.
11th and 12th rows In 1st C, K.
13th row In 2nd C, K2, *sl1P, K1; rep from * to last st, K1.
14th row In 2nd C, K2, *yft, sl1P, yb, K1; rep from * to last st, K1.
15th and 16th rows In 1st C, K.
These 16 rows form patt.
Work straight in patt until Back measures 20(24: 28:31:34)cm [8(9½:11:12¼:13¼)in] ending with right side facing for next row.
Cast off 4 sts at beg of next 2 rows. [41(45:51:55: 59)sts] **
Work straight until Back measures 34(39:43:47: 50)cm [13½(15¼:17:18½:19¾)in] ending with r.s. facing.
Shape shoulders by casting off 11(12:15:16:18)sts at beg of next 2 rows.
Leave rem 19(21:21:23:23)sts on a spare needle.

FRONT

Work as for Back from ** to **.
Work straight until armhole measures 9(10:10: 10:10)cm [3½(4:4:4:4)in], ending with r.s. facing.
Divide for neck, keeping patt correct, as folls:
Next row Patt 14(15:18:19:21), K2tog, turn and leave rem sts on a spare needle.
Dec 1 st at neck edge on every row until 11(12: 15:16:18)sts rem.
Work a few rows straight until Front matches Back to shoulder, ending with r.s. facing.
Cast off rem sts.
With r.s. facing, slip centre 9(11:11:13:13)sts on a length of yarn, rejoin yarn to rem sts, K2tog, patt to end.
Work to match first side, reversing shapings.

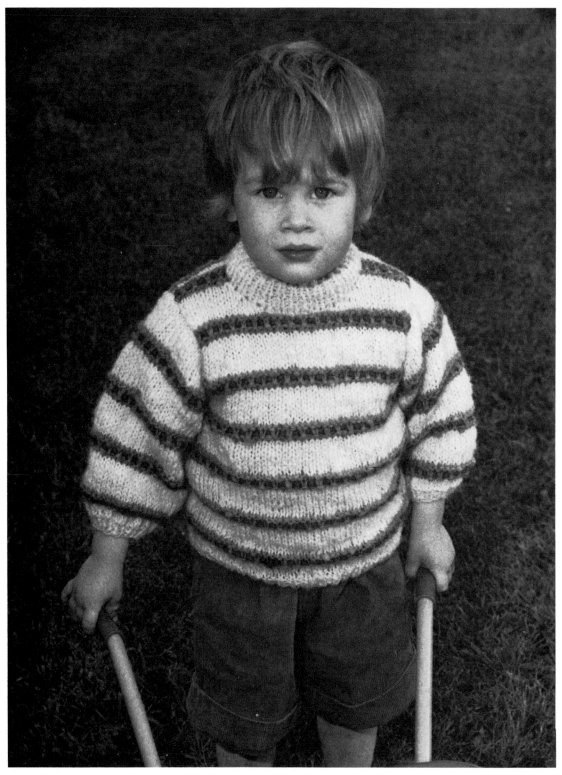

18 Joseph

SLEEVES

With 4mm needles and MS, cast on 28(30:30:32:34)sts and work in K1, P1 rib for 3cm [1¼in].

Next row Rib 3(3:4:4:5), M1, [rib 1, M1] 22(24:24:24:24) times, rib 3(3:4:4:5), [51(55:55:57:59)sts]

Change to 5mm needles and work in patt as given for Back until sleeve measures 25(27:31:35:39)cm [9¾(10½:12¼:13¾:15¼)in], ending with r.s. facing.

Place markers at each end of last row.

Work a further 6 rows in patt.

Cast off.

MAKE UP AND NECK BORDER

Press lightly on w.s. using a warm iron and a damp cloth.

Join right shoulder seam.

NECK BORDER

With r.s. facing, 4mm needles and MS, *Knit up* 12(12:12:14:14)sts down left side of neck, K9(11:11:13:13)sts from front, *Knit up* 12(12:12:14:14)sts up right side of neck, K19(21:21:23:23)sts from back. [52(56:56:64:64)sts]

Work in K1, P1 rib for 5(5:6:6:6)cm [2(2:2¼:2¼:2¼)in].

Using a 5mm needle, cast off loosely in rib.

Join left shoulder and Neck Border.

Fold Neck Border in half to w.s. and slip-hem loosely in position.

Placing centre of sleeves to shoulders, sew in position between markers.

Join side and sleeve seams.

Press seams.

Sarah

Breed: Romney
Category; Longwool and Lustre

Brightly coloured bobbles are displayed at their best nestling amongst the lacey Vees in the yoke and sleeves of this girl's sweater, on a background of soft creamy Romney.

MATERIALS

Hand Spun – Romney and Worsted Tops
7 threads per cm – Single ply
17 threads per in – Single ply

Commercial Equivalent – Aran type (thick)
4 threads per cm
10 threads per in

275(300:325:350)g of Main Shade, oddments in Contrasts,
Pair each 4mm and 5mm knitting needles.
NB If using a commercial yarn allow extra.

MEASUREMENTS

To fit chest 56(61:66:71)cm [22(24:26:28)in].
Length from top of shoulders approx 38(42:46:49)cm [15(16½:18:19¼)in].
Sleeve seam 23(27:31:35)cm [9(10½:12¼:13¾)in].

TENSION

18 sts and 24 rows to 10cm [4in] measured over stocking stitch on 5mm needles.

SPECIAL ABBREVIATIONS

MB = make bobble by working K1, P1, K1, P1, K1 into next st, turn, K5, turn, P5, turn, K2tog, K1, K2tog, turn, P3tog, thus completing bobble.
MS = Main Shade; C = Contrast.

NOTE

When working bobbles in contrasting colours, you may use as many or as few colours as you desire, in whatever way you wish.

MOTIF (7 sts)

1st row In MS, K2, sl1, K1, yfwd, K1, psso, K2.
2nd and every alt row In MS, P.
3rd row In MS, K1, K2tog, yfwd, K1, yfwd, sl1, K1, psso, K1.
5th row In MS, K2tog, yfwd, K3, yfwd, sl1, K1, psso.
7th row K3MS, MB in C, K3MS.
8th row As 2nd.
These 8 rows form motif.

FRONT

**With 4mm needles and MS, cast on 48(52:56:60)sts and work in K1, P1 rib for 3(3:4:4)cm [1¼(1¼:1½:1½)in].
Next row Rib 4(6:6:6), M1, [rib 10(10:11:12), M1] 4 times, rib 4(6:6:6). [53(57:61:65)sts]
Change to 5mm needles and work in st.st. until Front measures 11(16:19.5:22.5)cm [4¼(6¼:7¾:9)in], ending with a P row.**
Commence yoke as folls:

1ST SIZE
1 row K23, Motif 7 sts as 1st row, K23.
2nd row P23, Motif 7 sts as 2nd row, P23.
Work 6 rows as set, working appropriate rows of motif.
9th row K15, [Motif 7 sts as 1st row, K1] 3 times, K14.
10th row P15, [Motif 7 sts as 2nd row, P1] 3 times, P14.
Work 4 rows as set, working appropriate rows of motifs.
Shape armholes as folls:
15th row Cast off 3 sts, K12, [Motif 7 sts as 7th row, K1] 3 times, K14.
16th row Cast off 3 sts, P12, [Motif 7 sts as 8th row, P1] 3 times, P12.
17th row K2tog, K2, [Motif 7 sts as 1st row, K1] 5 times, K1, K2tog.
18th row P3, [Motif 7 sts as 2nd row, P1] 5 times, P3.
Rep last 2 rows twice more, working appropriate rows of motif and dec as given. [41sts]

2ND SIZE
1st row K25, Motif 7 sts as 1st row, K25.
2nd row P25, Motif 7 sts as 2nd row, P25.

19 Sarah

Work 6 rows as set, working appropriate rows of motif.

Shape armholes as folls:

9th row Cast off 3 sts, K14, [Motif 7 sts as 1st row, K1] 3 times, K16.

10th row Cast off 3 sts, P14, [Motif 7 sts as 2nd row, P1] 3 times, P13.

11th row K2tog, K12, [Motif 7 sts as 3rd row, K1] 3 times, K11, K2tog.

12th row P13, [Motif 7 sts as 4th row, P1] 3 times, P12.

Rep last 2 rows twice more, working appropriate rows of motif and dec as given until 45 sts rem.

Next row K2tog, K1, [Motif 7 sts as 1st row, K1] 5 times, K2tog.

Next row P2, [Motif 7 sts as 2nd row, P1] 5 times, P1. [43 sts].

3RD SIZE

1st row K28, Motif 7 sts as 1st row, K28.

2nd row P28, Motif 7 sts as 2nd row, P28.

Work 4 more rows as set, working appropriate rows of motif.

Shape armholes as folls:

7th row Cast off 3 sts, K25, Motif 7 sts as 7th row, K28.

8th row Cast off 3 sts, P25, Motif 7 sts as 8th row, P25.

9th row K2tog, K13, [Motif 7 sts as 1st row, K2] 3 times, K11, K2tog.

10th row P14, [Motif 7 sts as 2nd row, P2] 3 times, P12.

Rep last 2 rows 3 times more, working appropriate rows of motif and dec as given. [47sts]

17th row K2tog, [Motif 7 sts as 1st row, K2] 4 times, Motif 7 sts as 1st row, K2tog.

18th row P1, [Motif 7 sts as 2nd row, P2] 4 times, Motif 7 sts as 2nd row, P1. [45sts]

4TH SIZE

1st row K29, Motif 7 sts as 1st row, K29.

2nd row P29, Motif 7 sts as 2nd row, P29.

Work 2 rows as set, working appropriate rows of motif.

Shape armholes as folls:

5th row Cast off 3 sts, K26, Motif 7 sts as 5th row, K29.

6th row Cast off 3 sts, P26, Motif 7 sts as 6th row, P26.

7th row K2tog, K24, Motif 7 sts as 7th row, K24, K2tog.

8th row P25, Motif 7 sts as 8th row, P25.

9th row K2tog, K14, [Motif 7 sts as 1st row, K2] times, K12, K2tog.

10th row P15, [Motif 7 sts as 2nd row, P2] 3 times, P13.

Rep last 2 rows 3 times more, working appropriate rows of motif and dec as given. [49sts]

17th row K3, [Motif 7 sts as 1st row, K2] 5 times, K1.

18th row P3, [Motif 7 sts as 2nd row, P2] 5 times, P1.

ALL SIZES

Work straight in patt as set for a further 6(10:8:8) more rows.

Divide for neck, keeping patt correct, as folls:

Next row Patt 14(15:16:17), K2tog, turn and leave rem sts on a spare needle.

Work 1 row.

Dec 1 st at neck edge on every alt row until 12(12:12:13)sts rem.

Work 5(3:5:3) rows.

Shape shoulders by casting off 6 sts at beg of next row. Work 1 row.

Cast off rem 6(6:6:7)sts.

With r.s. facing, slip centre 9(9:11:11)sts on a length of yarn, rejoin yarn to rem sts, K2tog, patt to end.

Work to match first side, reversing shapings.

BACK

Work as for Front from ** to **.

Work straight until Back matches Front to armhole ending with r.s. facing.

Shape armholes by casting off 3 sts at beg of next 2 rows.

Dec 1 st at each end of next and every foll alt row until 41(43:45:49)sts rem.

Work straight until Back matches Front to shoulder, ending with r.s. facing.

Shape shoulders by casting off 6 sts at beg of next 2 rows, then 6(6:6:7)sts at beg of foll 2 rows.

Leave rem 17(19:21:23)sts on a spare needle.

SLEEVES

With 4mm needles and MS, cast on 32(32:34:36)sts and work in K1, P1 rib for 3cm [1¼in].

Next row Rib 4(4:5:6), M1, [rib 3, M1] 8 times, rib 4(4:5:6). [41(41:43:45)sts]

Change to 5mm needles and work 2 rows in st.st.

Place motifs as folls:

1st row K1 (1:2:1), [Motif 7 sts as 1st row, K1 (1:1:2)] 4 times, Motif 7 sts as 1st row, K1 (1:2:1).

2nd row P1 (1:2:1), [Motif 7 sts as 2nd row, P1 (1:1:2)] 4 times, Motif 7 sts as 2nd row, P1 (1:2:1).

Work 6 more rows as set.

Cont in st.st. until sleeves measures 23(27:31:35)cm [9(10½:12¼:13¾)in], ending with a P row.

Shape top by casting off 3 sts at beg of next 2 rows.

Dec 1 st at each end of next and every alt row until 23(15:15:15)sts rem, ending with r.s. facing.

1ST SIZE

Dec 1 st at each end of every row until 15 sts rem.

ALL SIZES

Cast off.

MAKE UP AND NECK BORDER

Join right shoulder seam.

Neck Border

With 4mm needles and MS, *Knit up* 11(11:13:13)sts down left side of neck, K9(9:11:11)sts from front, *Knit up* 11(11:13:13)sts up right side of neck, K17(19:21:23)sts from back. [48(50:58:60)sts]

Work in K1, P1 rib for 5cm [2in].

Using a 5mm needle, cast off loosely in rib.

Join left shoulder and Neck Border.

Fold Neck Border in half to w.s. and slip-hem loosely in position.

Join side and sleeve seams.

Insert sleeves.

Press seams.

Rosetta

Breed: Swalesdale Lambswool
Category: Mountain and Hill
Other fibre: Silk

A colourful waistcoat, created by blending vivid red and blue commercially dyed yarns with a white lambswool/mohair mixture to give a deep mauve effect. The contrasting stripes which are threaded with red velvet ribbons are of one strand of the above mixture and one strand of silk waste, plyed together.

NOTE

It is important to blend the red/blue together first to obtain mauve. Then by laying a thin layer of mauve on the carders, followed by a layer of mohair and lastly the white lambswool, the yarn is ready for carding and blending in the usual way. It is also very important when colour blending to ensure that the blending is done in one session as continuity is important. To go back later and finish blending might give a completely different colour.

Breakdown of mixture: Mohair – 40g; Lambswool – 40g; Red – 10g; Blue – 10g.

MATERIALS

Hand Spun – Swaledale Lambswool
9 threads per cm – Single ply
22 threads per in – Single ply

Silk Waste
9 threads per cm – Single ply
22 threads per in – Single ply

Commercial Equivalent – Double Knitting (thick)
5 threads per cm
12 threads per in

250(275:300:350:375)g of Main Shade.
50g of Contrast.

Pair each 4mm and 5½mm knitting needles. A 4mm crochet hook.
9(10:11:12:13) metres of narrow velvet ribbon.
7 Buttons.
NB If using a commercial yarn allow extra.

MEASUREMENTS

To fit bust 81(86:91:97:102)cm [32(34:36:38:40)in].
Length from top of shoulders 56(56:57:58:58)cm. [22(22:22½:22¾:22¾)in].

TENSION

18 sts and 27 rows to 10cm [4in] measured over pattern on 5½mm needles.

SPECIAL ABBREVIATIONS

MS = Main Shade; C = Contrast.

BACK AND FRONTS (worked in one piece to armhole)

With 4mm needles and MS, cast on 147(155:163:171:179)sts and work in rib as folls:
1st row K2, * P1, K1; rep from * to last st, K1.
2nd row K1, * P1, K1; rep from * to end.
Rep these 2 rows for 6cm [2¼in], ending with 2nd row.
Change to 5½mm needles and joining in C as required, work in patt as folls:
1st and 2nd row In C, K.
3rd row In C, K2, * yfwd, K2tog; rep from * to last st, K1.
4th row In C, K.
5th row In MS, K.
6th row In MS, P.
7th row In MS, K3, * K2tog, yfwd, K1, yfwd, sl1 K, K1, psso, K3; rep from * to end.
8th row In MS, P2, * P2togtbl, yrn, P3, yrn, P2tog, P1; rep from * to last st, P1.
9th row In MS, K1, K2tog, * yfwd, K5, yfwd, sl1 K, K2tog, psso; rep from * to last 8 sts, yfwd, K5, yfwd, sl1, K1, psso, K1.
10th row In MS, P2, * yrn, P2tog, P3, P2togtbl, yrn, P1; rep from * to last st, P1.

20 Rosetta

11th row In MS, K3, * yfwd, sl1, K1, psso, K1, K2tog, yfwd, K3; rep from * to end.

12th row In MS, P4, * yrn, sl1P, P2tog, psso, yrn, P5; rep from * to last 7 sts, yrn, sl1P, P2tog, psso, yrn, P4.

These 12 rows form patt.

Work straight in patt until Back measures approx 38cm [15in], ending with 12th row of patt.

Divide for armholes, keeping patt correct, as folls:

Next row K33(35:37:39:41), cast off 8 sts, K65(69:73:77:81)sts including st on needle after cast off, cast off 8 sts, K to end.

Cont on last group of 33(35:37:39:41)sts for Left Front.

Work straight until armhole measures 9(9:10:11: 10)cm [3½(3½:4:4¼::4)in], ending with r.s. facing.

Shape front neck, keeping patt correct, as folls:

Next row Patt to last 6(6:6:7:7)sts, turn and leave these sts on a safety-pin.

Dec 1 st at neck edge on next and every foll alt row until 19(21:22:23:24)sts rem.

Work straight until armhole measures 18(18:19: 20:20)cm [7(7:7½:8:8)in], ending with r.s. facing. Cast off rem sts.

With w.s. facing, rejoin appropriate colour to sts for Back.

Work straight in patt until Back matches Front to shoulder, ending with r.s. facing.

Cast off 19(21:22:23:24)sts at beg of next 2 rows.

Leave rem 27(27:29:31:33)sts on a spare needle.

With w.s. facing, rejoin appropriate colour to sts for Right Front.

Complete to match Left Front, reversing shapings.

MAKE UP AND BORDERS

Join shoulder seams.

Neck Border

With r.s. facing, 4mm needles and MS, K6(6:6:7: 7)sts from safety-pin, *Knit up* 16(16:16:16:19)sts up right side of neck, K27(27:29:31:33)sts from back, *Knit up* 16(16:16:16:19)sts down left side of neck, K6(6:6:7:7)sts from safety-pin. [71(71:73: 77:85)sts].

Work in rib as given for lower edge, starting with 2nd row, for 9 rows.

Cast off evenly in rib.

Buttonhole Border

With r.s. facing, 4mm needles and MS, starting at lower edge of Right Front, *Knit up* 99(99:101: 101:101)sts to top of Neck Border.

Starting with 2nd row, work in rib as given for lower edge for 3 rows.

Next row (Buttonhole row), rib 4(4:5:5:5)sts, * cast off 2 sts, rib 13, including st on needle after cast off; rep from * to last 5(5:6:6:6)sts, cast off 2 sts, rib to end.

Next row Rib, casting on 2 sts over those cast off. Work 4 more rows in rib. Cast off evenly in rib.

Button Border

With r.s. facing, 4mm needles and MS, starting at top of Neck Border, *Knit up* 99(99:101:101: 101)sts down Left Front.

Work 9 rows in rib as given for lower edge, starting with 2nd row.

Cast off evenly in rib.

Armhole Borders

With r.s. facing, 4mm crochet hook and MS, work 1 row of dc all round armholes.

Thread ribbon through eyelets and secure on w.s.

Press seams.

Sew on buttons.

Louise

Breed: Shetland
Category: Shortwool and Down
Other Fibres: Silk; Dog hair

A subtle blend of colour, a touch of silk and a smattering of dog hair has been used to create this very pretty jumper. Despite its complicated appearance, it is knitted throughout in stocking stitch.

NOTE

Place on carders a very small amount of either blue, green, red or yellow worsted tops. Add a little white dog hair (or white mohair or angora) and blend with white Shetland. All four shades are plyed with silk waste.

MATERIALS

Shetland/Dog Hair

9 threads per cm – Single ply
22 threads per in – Single ply

Silk Waste

9 threads per cm – Single ply
22 threads per in – Single ply

Commercial Equivalent

5 threads per cm
12 threads per in

275(325)g of Green, 150(175)g of Pink, 80(95)g of Blue and 80(95)g of Yellow.
Pair each 3¾mm and 4½mm knitting needles.
NB If using a commercial yarn allow extra.

MEASUREMENTS

To fit bust 81–86(91–97)cm [32–34(36–38)in].
Length from top of shoulders 60(61)cm [23½(24)in].
Sleeve seam 46cm [18in].

TENSION

22 sts and 26 rows to 10cm [4in] measured over stocking stitch on 4½mm needles.

SPECIAL ABBREVIATIONS

G = Green; P = Pink; B = Blue; Y = Yellow.

BACK

With 4½mm needles and P, cast on 54(63)sts loosely.
Work base triangles as folls:
*P1, turn, K1, turn, P2, turn, K2, turn, P3, turn, K3, turn, P4, turn, K4, turn, P5, turn, K5, turn, P6, turn, K6, turn, P7, turn, K7, turn, P8, turn, K8, turn, P9, turn, K9, turn, P9, * there are now 9 sts on right hand needle (1st triangle formed); rep from * to *, there are now 18 sts on right hand needle (2 triangles formed).
Cont thus until 6(7) triangles in all have been formed, turn.
Base triangles are now complete. Break P.

**Join in B, and work across set of 9 sts just worked as folls:
K2, turn, P2, turn, inc in first st, sl1 K, K1, psso, turn, P3, turn, inc in first st, K1, sl1 K, K1, psso, turn, P4, inc in first st, K2, sl1, K1, psso, turn, P5, turn, inc in first st, K3, sl1 K, K1, psso, turn, P6, inc in first st, K4, sl1 K, K1, psso, turn, P7, turn, inc in first st, K5, sl1 K, K1, psso, turn, P8, turn, inc in first st, K6, sl1 K, K1, psso.
*Using same needle, *Knit up* 9 sts down left side of triangle, turn, P9, turn, K8, sl1 K, K1, (first st of next triangle), psso, [turn, P9, turn, K8, sl1 K, K1, psso] 8 times, rep from * to last triangle, *Knit up* 9 sts down left side of last triangle, turn, P2tog, P7, turn, K8, turn, P2tog, P6, turn, K7, turn, P2tog, P5, turn, K6, turn, P2tog, P4, K5, turn, P2tog, P3, turn, K4, turn, P2tog, P2, turn, K3, turn, P2tog, P1, turn, K2, turn, P2tog, turn, K1, turn, P1. Break B.***

Join in G and using same needle as last st worked, pick up and P8 sts down left side of triangle just completed, * [turn, K9, turn, P8, P2tog] 9 times.

21 Louise

Using G, pick up and P9 sts down left side of foll
  rectangle.
Rep from * to end, turn. Break G.**
Rep from ** to ** 5 times more, then rep from ** to
  *** once more, rotating colours as folls: Y; P; B;
  G; Y; P; B; G; Y; P; and B.
Join in G and work as folls:
*pick up and P9 sts down side of last triangle (10
  sts in all), turn, K10, turn, P2tog, P7, P2tog,
  (working last st of those picked up along with 1st
  stitch from foll rectangle), turn, K9, turn, P2tog,
  P6, P2tog, turn, K8, turn, P2tog, P5, P2tog, turn,
  K7, turn, P2tog, P4, P2tog, turn, K6, turn, P2tog,
  P3, P2tog, turn, K5, turn, P2tog, P2, P2tog, turn,
  K4, turn, P2tog, P1, P2tog, turn, K3, turn,
  [P2tog] twice, turn, K2, turn, P3tog; rep from * to
  end. Do not break G.
Work a second piece for Front.

BACK YOKE

With right side facing, 4½mm needles and using G,
  Knit up 96(112)sts along top edge.
Starting with a P row, work in st.st. for 19 rows.
Cast off 28(34)sts at beg of next 2 rows.
Leave rem 40(44)sts on a spare needle.

LOWER EDGE BORDER

With r.s. facing, 3¾mm needles and using P, *Knit
  up* 84(98)sts along lower edge.
Work in K1, P1 rib for 3(4)cm [1¼(1½)in].
Cast off neatly in rib.

FRONT
Work as for Back.

FRONT YOKE

With r.s. facing, 4½mm needles and using G, *Knit
  up* 96(112)sts along top edge.
Starting with a P row, work in st.st. for 3 rows.
Divide for neck as folls:

Next row K34(40), K2tog, turn and leave rem sts
  on a spare needle.
Dec 1 st at neck edge on every row until 28(34)sts
  rem.
Work a few rows straight until Front matches
  Back to shoulder, ending with r.s. facing.
Cast off rem sts.
With r.s. facing, slip centre 24(28)sts on a length of
  yarn, rejoin yarn to rem sts, K2tog, K to end.
Work to match first side, reversing shapings.

LOWER EDGE BORDER

Work as for Lower Edge Border on Back.

SLEEVES

With 3¾mm needles and G, cast on 46(50)sts and
  work in K1, P1 rib for 3cm [1¼ in].
Next row Rib 2, M1, [rib 1, M1] 41(45) times, rib
  3. [88(96)sts]
Change to 4½ *needles* and work in st.st. until sleeve
  measures 46cm [18in], ending with a P row.
Cast off.

MAKE UP AND NECK BORDER

Join right shoulder seams.

Neck Border
With 3¾mm needles and G, *Knit up* 16 sts down left
  side of neck, K24(28)sts from front, *Knit up* 16 sts
  up right side of neck, K40(44)sts from back.
  [96(104)sts]
Work in K1, P1 rib for 6cm [2¼in].
Using a 4½mm needle, cast off loosely in rib.
Join left shoulder and Neck Border.
Fold Neck Border in half to w.s. and slip-hem
  loosely in position.
Place centre of sleeve to shoulder and sew in down
  side edges of Front and Back.
Join side and sleeve seams.
Press seams.

Ivy

Category: Commercially Dyed Worsted Tops

Bright yellow and vivid red blended together to arrive at flame in all its splendour was used to make this stunning but simple bomber jacket.

MATERIALS

Hand Spun – Worsted Tops
5.5 threads per cm – Single ply
13 threads per in – Single ply

Commercial Equivalent – Chunky
3 threads per cm
7/8 threads per in

650(700:750:800)g of Wool.
Pair each $5\frac{1}{2}$mm and $6\frac{1}{2}$mm knitting needles.
7 Buttons.
NB If using a commercial yarn allow extra.

MEASUREMENTS

To fit bust 76(81:86:91)cm [30(32:34:36)in].
Length from top of shoulders 52(53:54:55)cm [$20\frac{1}{2}(21:21\frac{1}{4}:21\frac{3}{4})$in].
Sleeve seam 39(43:43:44)cm [$15\frac{1}{4}(17:17:17\frac{1}{4})$in].

TENSION

13 sts and 18 rows to 10cm [4in] measured over stocking stitch on $6\frac{1}{2}$mm needles.

BACK

With $5\frac{1}{2}$mm needles, cast on 47(49:53:55)sts and work in rib as folls:
1st row (R.S.), K2, * P1, K1; rep from * to last st, K1.
2nd row K1, * P1, K1; rep from * to end.
Rep these 2 rows until rib measures 6cm [$2\frac{1}{4}$in], ending with 1st row.
Next row Rib 3(4:4:5), M1, [rib 8(8:9:9), M1] 5 times, rib to end. [53(55:59:63)sts]
Change to $6\frac{1}{2}$mm needles and starting with a K row, work in st.st. until Back measures 34cm [$13\frac{1}{2}$in], ending with a P row.
Shape raglans by casting off 3(3:4:4)sts at beg of next 2 rows.

2ND, 3RD AND 4TH SIZES
Dec 1 st at each end of next row. Work 3 rows.

ALL SIZES
Dec 1 st at each end of next and every foll alt row until 17(19:19:21)sts rem, ending with a P row.
Leave rem sts on a spare needle.

LEFT FRONT

With $5\frac{1}{2}$mm needles, cast on 31(33:35:37)sts and work in rib as given for Back for 6cm [$2\frac{1}{4}$in], ending with 1st row.
Next row Rib 11(11:11:13), [M1 rib 10(11:12:12)] 2 times. [33(35:37:39)sts]
Change to $6\frac{1}{2}$mm needles and work as folls:
1st row K26(28:30:32), rib 7.
2nd row Rib 7, P to end.
Cont thus working until Front matches Back to start of raglan shaping, ending with r.s. facing.
Shape raglan by casting off 3(3:4:4)sts at beg of next row. Work 1 row.

2ND, 3RD AND 4TH SIZES
Dec 1 st at beg of next row. Work 3 rows.

ALL SIZES
Dec 1 st at beg of next and at same edge on every foll alt row until 20(22:22:23)sts rem ending with r.s. facing.
Shape neck as folls:
Next row K2tog, K9(11:11:12), K2tog, turn and leave rem 7 sts on a safety-pin.
Dec 1 st at neck edge on every row at the same time dec 1 st at raglan on every alt row until 4(3:3:2)sts rem, ending with r.s. facing.
Dec 1 st at raglan *only* as before until 2 sts rem, ending with r.s. facing.
Next row K2tog and fasten off.
Mark positions for 6 buttons evenly spaced along front rib band, with the 7th button for Neck Band.

22 Ivy

RIGHT FRONT

With 5½mm needles, cast on 31(33:35:37)sts and
work in rib as given for Back, for 4 rows.

Buttonhole row (R.S.), Rib 3, cast off 2 sts, patt to
end.

Next row Patt casting on 2 sts over those cast off.
Cont in rib until work measures 6cm [2¼in], ending
with w.s. facing.

Next row [Rib 10(11:12:12), M1] 2 times, rib to
end. [33(35:37:39)sts]

Change to 6½mm needles and keeping first 7 sts in
rib, work as for Left Front, reversing shapings and
forming rem buttonholes opposite markers.

SLEEVES

With 5½mm needles, cast on 28(28:30:30)sts and
work in K1, P1 rib for 5cm [2in].

Next row Rib 3(3:4:4), M1, [rib 7, M1] 3 times,
rib to end. [32(32:34:34)sts]

Change to 6½mm needles and work in st.st.
shaping sides by inc 1 st at each end of 5th and
every foll 8th row until there are 40(42:44:46)sts.

Work straight until sleeve measures 39(43:43:
44)cm [15¼(17:17:17¼)in], ending with r.s. facing.

Shape raglans by casting off 3(3:4:4)sts at beg of
next 2 rows.

Dec 1 st at each end of next row. Work 3 rows.

4TH SIZE
Rep last 4 rows once more.

ALL SIZES
Dec 1 st at each end of next and every foll alt row
until 6 sts rem, ending with r.s. facing.
Leave rem sts on a spare needle.

MAKE UP AND NECKBAND

Join raglans, side and sleeve seams.

Neck Band

With r.s. facing, 5½mm needles, rib across 7 sts
from right front, *Knit up* 9 sts up right side of
neck, K6 sts from sleeve, K17(19:19:21)sts from
back, K6 sts from sleeve, *Knit up* 9 sts down left
side of neck, rib 7 sts from left front. [61(63:63:
65)sts]

Work in rib for 3cm [1¼in], making 7th buttonhole
at centre of band.

Cast off in rib.

Press seams.

Sew on buttons.

Morwenna

Breed: Romney
Category: Longwool and Lustre
Other fibres: Goat hair

Softness is the theme of this drop-shoulder, slash-neck sweater with its attractive cables. The main shade was a blend of two-thirds Romney with one-third Mohair. The pale pink, blue and lilac of the cables were obtained by blending Romney and Mohair with just a touch of worsted tops for a hint of colour.

MATERIALS

Hand Spun – Romney, Mohair and Worsted Tops
9 threads per cm – Single ply
22 threads per in – Single ply

Commercial Equivalent – Double Knitting (thick)
5 threads per cm
12 threads per in

300(325:350:375)g of Main Shade, 20(20:20:25)g of A, 20(20:20:25)g of B and 20(20:20:25)g of C. Pair each 3¼mm and 4mm needles. Cable needle. NB If using a commercial yarn allow extra.

MEASUREMENTS

To fit bust 81(86:91:97)cm [32(34:36:38)in].
Length from top of shoulders 48(49:50:51)cm [19(19¼:19¾:20)in].
Sleeve seam 46cm [18in].

TENSION

22 sts and 30 rows to 10cm [4in] measured over stocking stitch on 4mm needles.

SPECIAL ABBREVIATIONS

C8F = slip next 4 sts onto cable needle and leave at front of work, K4, then K4 from cable needle.
MS = Main Shade.

PANEL PATTERN (12 sts)
1st and 3rd rows P2, K8, P2.
2nd and every alt row K2, P8, K2.
5th row P2, C8F, P2.
7th row As 1st.
8th row As 2nd.
These 8 rows form panel patt.

NOTE

Do not carry colours across w.s. of work, but use separate balls of MS and contrasts as required, twisting yarns on w.s. when changing colour to avoid a hole and taking yarn back and forward as required.

BACK AND FRONT (ALIKE)

With 3¼mm needles and MS, cast on 94(100: 106:112)sts and work in K1, P1 rib for 8cm [3¼in].
Next row Rib 5(8:7:7), M1 [rib 12(12:13:14), M1] 7 times, rib to end. [102(108:114:120)sts]
Change to 4mm needles and joining in colours as required, work in st.st. placing panels as folls:
1st row K16(18:21:23)MS, Panel Patt 12 sts as 1st row in A, Panel Patt 12 sts as 1st row in B, Panel Patt 12 sts as 1st row in C, K to end in MS.
2nd row P50(54:57:61)MS, Panel Patt as 2nd row in C, Panel Patt as 2nd row in B, Panel Patt as 2nd row in A, P to end in MS.
Cont thus working appropriate rows of panel patt until 16 rows have been worked in all.
Next row K16(18:21:23)MS, Panel Patt 12 sts in A, Panel Patt 12 sts in B, K to end in MS.
Next row P62(66:69:73)MS, Panel Patt 12 sts in B, Panel Patt 12 sts in A, P to end in MS.
Work 6 more rows as set.
Next row K16(18:21:23)MS, Panel Patt 12 sts in A, K to end in MS.
Next row P74(78:81:85)MS, Panel Patt 12 sts in A, P to end in MS.
Work 6 more rows as set.
Cont in MS *only* in st.st. until Back measures 34(35:36:37)cm [13½(13¾:14¼:14½)in], ending with r.s. facing.
Next row K74(78:81:85)MS, Panel Patt 12 sts as 1st row in A, K to end in MS.

23 Morwenna

Next row P16(18:21:23)MS, Panel Patt 12 sts as 2nd row in A, P to end in MS.

Work 6 rows as set.

Next row K62(66:69:73)MS, Panel Patt 12 sts as 1st row in B, Panel Patt 12 sts in A, K to end in MS.

Next row P16(18;21;23)MS, Panel Patt 12 sts in A, Panel Patt 12 sts in B, P to end in MS.

Work 6 rows as set.

Next row K50(54:57:61)MS, Panel Patt 12 sts as 1st row in C, Panel Patt 12 sts in B, Panel Patt 12 sts in A, K to end in MS.

Next row P16(18:21:23)MS, Panel Patt 12 sts in A, Panel Patt 12 sts in B, Panel Patt 12 sts in C, P to end in MS.

Work 14 rows as set.

Inc 1 st at beg of next row, K 1 row. [103(109: 115:121)sts]

Work in P1, K1 rib, rows on w.s. having a P1 at each end, for 3cm [1¼in], ending with r.s. facing.

Cast off.

SLEEVES

With 3¼mm needles and MS, cast on 48(50:50: 52)sts and work in K1, P1 rib for 5cm [2in].

Next row Rib 6, M1, [rib 1, M1] 35(37:37:39) times, rib 7. [84(88:88:92)sts]

Change to 4mm needles and joining in colours as required, work in st.st. placing panels as folls:

1st row K12(13:13:14)MS, Panel Patt 12sts as 1st row in A, Panel Patt 12 sts as 1st row in B, Panel Patt 12 sts as 1st row in C, K to end in MS.

2nd row P36(39:39:42)MS, Panel Patt 12 sts as 2nd row in C, Panel Patt 12 sts as 2nd row in B, Panel Patt 12 sts as 2nd row in A, P to end in MS.

Work 14 rows as set.

Next row K12(13:13:14)MS, Panel Patt 12 sts in A, Panel Patt 12 sts in B, K to end in MS.

Next row P48(51:51:54)MS, Panel Patt 12 sts in B, Panel Patt 12 sts in A, P to end in MS.

Work 6 more rows as set.

Next row K12(13:13:14)MS, Panel Patt 12 sts in A, K to end in MS.

Next row P60(63:63:66)MS, Panel Patt 12 sts in A, P to end in MS.

Work 6 rows as set.

Cont in MS *only* in st.st. until sleeve measures 46cm [18in], ending with right side facing.

Cast off.

MAKE UP

Join shoulders, leaving a gap of 22cm [8¾in] at centre for head.

Measure down 19(20:20:21)cm [7½(8:8:8¼in] from each shoulder on Back and Front.

Place markers. Sew sleeves in between markers.

Join side and sleeve seams.

Penelope

Category: Shortwool and Down
Breed: Lambswool
Other Fibres: Silk

This simple lace and moss stitch sweater has been created by using a small quantity of vivid red commercially dyed yarn, blended down to the palest pink and plyed with pure silk waste and finally threaded with slightly darker pink ribbon.

MATERIALS

Hand Spun – Lambswool
8 threads per cm – Single ply
20 threads per in – Single ply

Hand Spun – Silk
8 threads per cm – Single ply
20 threads per in – Single ply

Commercial Equivalent – Aran type (thin)
4.5 threads per cm
11 threads per in

450(475:500:525)g of Lambswool and Silk.
13(14:15:16) metres of narrow matching ribbon.
Pair each 3¾mm and 4½mm knitting needles.
NB If using a commercial yarn allow extra.

MEASUREMENTS

To fit bust 81(86:91:97)cm [32(34:36:38)in].
Length from top of shoulders 56(57:58:59)cm [22(22½:22¾::23¼)in].
Sleeve seam 46cm [18in].

TENSION

19 sts and 30 rows to 10cm [4in] measured over pattern on 4½mm needles.

BACK

**With 3¾mm needles, cast on 70(76:82:86)sts and work in K1, P1 rib for 6cm [2¼in].

Next row Rib 5(5:5:7), M1, [rib 10(11:12:12), M1] 6 times, rib 5(5:5:7). [77(83:89:93)sts]
Change to 4½mm needles and work in patt as folls:
1st–8th rows K1, * P1, K1; rep from * to end.
9th row K.
10th, 12th, 14th and 16th rows P.
11th row K3(2:1:2), * yfwd, sl1, K1, psso, K3, K2tog, yfwd, K1; rep from * to last 2(1:0:1)st, K2(1:0:1).
13th row K4(3:2:3), * yfwd, sl1, K1, psso, K1, K2tog, yfwd, K3; rep from * to last 9(8:7:8)sts, yfwd, sl1, K1, psso, K1, K2tog, yfwd, K4(3:2:3).
15th row K5(4:3:4), * yfwd, sl1, K2tog, psso, yfwd, K5; rep from * to last 8(7:6:7)sts, yfwd, sl1, K2tog, psso, yfwd, K5(4:3:4).
17th and 18th rows K.
19th row K2, * yfwd, K2tog; rep from * to last st, K1.
20th row K.
21st–28th rows As 9th–16th.
These 28 rows form patt.**
Work straight until Back measures 56(57:58: 59)cm [22(22½:22¾:23¼)in], ending with r.s. facing.
Cast off 24(27:29:30)sts at beg of next 2 rows.
Leave rem 29(29:31:33)sts on a spare needle.

FRONT

Work as for Back from ** to **.
Work straight in patt until Front measures 48(49: 50:51)cm [19(19¼:19¾:20)in], ending with r.s. facing.
Divide for neck, keeping patt correct as folls:
Next row Patt 29(32:35:36), K2tog, turn and leave rem sts on a spare needle.
Work 1 row.
Dec 1 st at neck edge on next and every alt row until 24(27:29:30)sts rem.
Work a few rows straight until Front matches Back to shoulder, ending with r.s. facing.
Cast off rem sts.
With r.s. facing, slip centre 15(15:15:17)sts on a length of yarn, rejoin yarn to rem sts, K2tog, patt to end.
Work to match first side, reversing shapings.

24 Penelope

SLEEVES

With 3¾mm needles, cast on 42(44:44:46)sts and work in K1, P1 rib for 7cm [2¾in].

Next row Rib 4(3:4:5), M1, [rib 1, M1] 34(38: 36:36) times, rib 4(3:4:5). [77(83:81:83)sts]

Change to 4½mm needles and work in patt as given for Back, until sleeve measures 46cm [18in], ending with r.s. facing.

Cast off.

MAKE UP AND NECK BORDER

Join right shoulder seam.

NECK BORDER

With r.s. facing, 3¾mm needles, *Knit up* 18 sts down left side of neck, K15(15:15:17)sts from centre, *Knit up* 18 sts up right side of neck, K29(29:31:33)sts from back. [80(80:82:86)sts]

Work in K1, P1 rib for 6cm [2¼in].

Using a 4½mm needle, cast off loosely in rib.

Join left shoulder and Neck Border.

Fold Neck Border in half to w.s. and slip-hem loosely in position.

Measure down 20(21:22:22)cm on side edges of Back and Front and place markers.

Placing centre of sleeve to shoulder, sew in sleeves between markers.

Join side and sleeve seams.

Press seams.

Thread ribbons through eyelets and secure on w.s. of work.

Commercial Dyeing (Yarns)

A very easy and reliable method of dyeing is to use commercial dyes in the form of kits obtainable from most craft shops, enabling the spinner to create her own colours for recording and future reference as we have done in the next design.

To give an example of recording, the following has been taken from our portfolio of the colours used in 'Petula'. There is approximately 120g (4oz) wool on each colour combination.

Basic Commercial Colours: Red   Blue   Black   Yellow

Dark Mauve	12ml red	24ml blue	
Light Mauve	18ml red	18ml blue	
Light Blue	24ml blue		
Grey	8ml black		
Light Pink	20ml red	4ml black	
Red	8ml yellow	64ml red	4ml blue
Green	20ml blue	20ml yellow	1ml black

We have attached all these shades against our recordings and are now in a position to obtain instant recall at any given time.

Petula

Breed: Jacob Lambswool
Category: Shortwool and Down
Other Fibre: Goat hair

As an easy and reliable method of dyeing, the spinner could use a commercial colour kit enabling her to create her own shades for recording and future reference as we have done with the coloured stripes in this sideways knitted coat: adding the slightest flecks of the coloured yarns to the main shade of black wool/mohair mixture.

Although we have used six contrasting colours in our coat, the design can be varied by using as many or as few colours as desired.

Wool mohair background – two-thirds wool to one-third mohair.

MATERIALS

Hand Spun – Jacob Lambswool, Mohair and Dorset Down
8 threads per cm – Single ply
20 threads per in – Single ply

Commercial Equivalent – Aran type (thin)
4.5 threads per cm
11 threads per in

350g of Main Shade and 40g of each of the six contrasting colours.
Pair $3\frac{3}{4}$mm knitting needles. Circular $4\frac{1}{2}$mm needle.
NB If using a commercial yarn allow extra.

MEASUREMENTS

One size: To fit bust 81–91cm [32–36in].
Length from top of shoulders 75cm [$29\frac{1}{2}$in].
Sleeve seam 46cm [18in].

TENSION

20 sts and 28 rows to 10cm [4in] measured over pattern on $4\frac{1}{2}$mm needles.

SPECIAL ABBREVIATIONS

MS = Main Shade; 1st C = 1st Contrast; 2nd C = 2nd Contrast; 3rd C = 3rd Contrast; 4th C = 4th Contrast; 5th C = 5th Contrast; 6th C = 6th Contrast.

STRIPE PATTERN

4 rows 1st C, 6 rows MS, 4 rows 2nd C, 6 rows MS, 4 rows 3rd C, 6 rows MS, 4 rows 4th C, 6 rows MS, 4 rows 5th C, 6 rows MS, 4 rows 6th C, 6 rows MS.
These 60 rows form stripe patt.

25 Petula

LEFT BACK, FRONT AND SLEEVE

(worked in one piece from centre back to wrist)

With circular 4½mm needle and MS, cast on 145 sts and P1 row.

1st row In 1st C, K2, * sl3, K1; rep from * to last 3 sts, K3.

2nd row In 1st C, P5, * sl1, P3; rep from * to end.

3rd row In 1st C, K.

4th row In 1st C, P.

5th row In MS, as 1st.

6th row In MS, as 2nd.

7th and 9th rows In MS, K.

8th and 10th rows In MS, P.

These 10 rows form patt.

Joining in and breaking off colours as required, work in patt and stripes as given for 26 rows.

Cast on 146 sts, patt across these sts, patt to end. [291 sts].

Cont in patt across all sts until 66 rows in all have been worked on Back section.

Keeping patt correct, cast off 108 sts at beg of next 2 rows. [75 sts].

Work straight in patt until sleeve measures 40cm [15¾in], ending with r.s. facing. Break all contrasts.

Change to 3¾mm needles and work as folls:

Next row K4 [K2tog] 33 times, K5. [42 sts].

Work in K1, P1 rib for 6cm [2¼in], ending with r.s. facing.

Cast off neatly in rib.

RIGHT BACK, FRONT AND SLEEVE

Work as for Left Back, Front and Sleeve, reversing shapings and working 1st and 2nd rows as folls:

1st row K4, * sl3, K1; rep from * to last st, K1.

2nd row *P3, sl1; rep from * to end, last 5 sts, P5.

MAKE UP AND BORDERS

Press lightly on w.s.

Join side and sleeve seams.

Lower Edge Rib

With r.s. facing, MS and 3¾mm needles, *Knit up* 163 sts around lower edge of coat.

Work in P1, K1 rib, rows on w.s. having a P1 at each end, for 2cm [¾in], ending with r.s. facing.

Cast off.

Front Border

With circular 4½mm needle, and MS, starting at lower edge of Right Front, *Knit up* 146 sts to shoulder, 49 sts across back neck, 146 sts to lower edge of Left Front. [341 sts].

1st row K1, * P1, K1; rep from * to end.

2nd row K2, * P1, K1; rep from * to last st, K1.

Rep these 2 rows for 9cm [3½in], ending with 1st row.

Cast off neatly in rib.

Press seams.

Commercial Dyeing (Garments)

As a third method of obtaining coloured garments try spinning the yarn and knitting the garment in the fleece's natural colour and then dyeing the whole garment after it has been completed. It doesn't even have to be a white fleece. Many a lovely shade has been obtained by using a Herdwick or Jacob fleece and then dyeing the garment, say, blue, maroon or any colour using the small packets of commercial wool dyes obtainable from most hardware shops.

It also takes a little of the worry out of natural dyeing. If the garment is completed, the concern about running out of the dyed yarn and not being able to obtain a true repeat to finish the garment has been eliminated. And, again, a little of the spun yarn added to the dye pot can give a record of the colour created for that portfolio!

Craig

Breed: Cheviot
Category: Mountain and Hill

Smart but casual man's V-neck cardigan in mainly stocking stitch with front Aran panels.

MATERIALS

Hand Spun – Cheviot
9 threads per cm – Single ply
22 threads per in – Single ply

Commercial Equivalent – Double Knitting (thick)
5 threads per cm
12 threads per in

500(550:600:650)g of Cheviot.
Pair each 3¼mm and 4mm knitting needles. Cable needle.
7 Buttons.
NB If using a commercial yarn allow extra.

MEASUREMENTS

To fit chest 97(102:107:112)cm [38(40:42:44)in].
Length from top of shoulders 63(65:66:67)cm [24¾(25½:26:26½)in].
Sleeve seam 46(47:47:48)cm [18(18½:18½:19)in].

TENSION

24 sts and 30 rows to 10cm [4in] measured over stocking stitch on 4mm needles.

SPECIAL ABBREVIATIONS

Tw2 = Twist 2 by knitting into front of 2nd st, then front of first st on left-hand needle and slipping 2 sts off needle together.
C4FP = Slip next 2 sts onto cable needle and leave at front of work, P2, then K2 from cable needle.
C4BP = Slip next 2 sts onto cable needle and leave at back of work, K2, then P2 from cable needle.
C4FK = Slip next 2 sts onto cable needle and leave at front of work, K2, then K2 from cable needle.
C4BK = Slip next 2 sts onto cable needle and leave at back of work, K2, then K2 from cable needle.

PANEL PATTERN (24 sts)

1st row P2, Tw2, P2, C4FP, C4FK, C4BP, P2, Tw2, P2.
2nd row K2, P2, K4, P8, K4, P2, K2.
3rd row P2, K2, P4, [C4BK] twice, P4, K2, P2.
4th row As 2nd.
5th row P2, Tw2, P2, C4BP, C4FK, C4FP, P2, Tw2, P2.
6th row [K2, P2] twice, K2, P4, K2, [P2, K2] twice.
7th row P2, K2, C4BP, P2, K4, P2, C4FP, K2, P2.
8th row K2, [P4, K4] twice, P4, K2.
9th row P2, C4FK, P4, K4, P4, C4FK, P2.
10th row As 8th.
11th row P2, K4, P4, C4FK, P4, K4, P2.
12th row As 8th.
13th row As 9th.
14th row As 8th.
15th row P2, K2, C4FP, P2, K4, P2, C4BP, K2, P2.
16th row As 6th.
These 16 rows form patt.

26 Craig

BACK

With 3¼mm needles, cast on 123(129:135:141)sts and work in K1, P1 rib, rows on r.s. having a K1 at each end, for 7cm [2¾in], ending with r.s. facing.

Change to 4mm needles and work in st.st. until Back measures 39cm [15¼in], ending with r.s. facing.

Shape armholes by casting off 5(6:7:8)sts at beg of next 2 rows, then dec 1 st at each end of next and every foll alt row until 93(97:101:105)sts rem.

Work straight until armhole measures 24(26:27:28)cm [9½(10¼:10½:11)in], ending with r.s. facing.

Shape shoulders by casting off 8(9:9:9)sts at beg of next 4 rows, then 9(8:9:10)sts at beg of foll 2 rows.

Cast off rem 43(45:47:49)sts.

POCKET LININGS (2)

With 4mm needles, cast on 30 sts and work in st.st. for 15 rows.

Next row P2, M1 [P5, M1] 5 times, P3. [36sts]

Leave sts on a spare needle.

LEFT FRONT

**With 3¼mm needles, cast on 61(65:67:71)sts and work in rib as given for Back, ending with w.s. facing.

Next row Rib 5(6:6:7), M1, [rib 10(13:11:14), M1] 5(4:5:4) times, rib to end. [67(70:73:76) sts]**

Change to 4mm needles and work in st.st. *placing panel* as folls:

1st row K19(20:22:23), Panel Patt as 1st row, K to end.

2nd row P24(26:27:29), Panel Patt as 2nd row, P to end.

Cont thus working appropriate rows of panel, until 16 rows in all have been worked.

Place pocket as folls:

Next row K13(14:16:17), slip next 36 sts on a length of yarn and in place of these patt across 36 sts of first Pocket Lining, K to end.

Cont in st.st. and panel patt until Front matches Back to armhole, ending with r.s. facing.

Shape armhole and *front slope* as folls:

Next row Cast off 5(6:7:8)sts, patt to last 2 sts, K2tog.

Work 1 row.

Dec 1 st at armhole edge on next and every alt row *at the same time* dec 1 st at front slope on every 3rd row from previous dec until 45(47:49:51)sts rem.

Cont dec at front slope *only* on every 3rd row as before until 31(32:33:34)sts rem.

Work straight until Front matches Back to shoulder, ending with r.s. facing.

Shape shoulder by casting off 10(11:11:11)sts at beg of next and foll alt row.

Work 1 row. Cast off rem 11(10:11:12)sts.

RIGHT FRONT

Work as for Left Front from ** to **.

Change to 4mm needles and work in st.st. *placing panel* as folls:

1st row K24(26:27:29), Panel Patt as 1st row, K to end.

2nd row P19(20:22:23), Panel Patt as 2nd row, P to end.

Cont thus working appropriate rows of panel, until 16 rows in all have been worked.

Place pocket as folls:

Next row K18(20:21:22), slip next 36 sts on a length of yarn and in place of these patt across 36 sts of second Pocket Lining, K to end.

Complete as for Left Front, reversing shapings.

SLEEVES

With 3¼mm needles, cast on 58(60:60:62)sts and work in K1, P1 rib for 6cm [2¼in].

Next row Rib 4(5:5:6), M1 [rib 10, M1] 5 times, rib to end. [64(66:66:68)sts]

Change to 4mm needles and work in st.st. shaping sides by inc 1 st at each end of 3rd and every foll 6th row until there are 96(98:100:104)sts.

Work straight until sleeve measures 46(47:47:48)cm [18(18½:18½:19)in], ending with r.s. facing.

Shape top by casting off 5(6:7:8)sts at beg of next 2 rows.

3RD AND 4TH SIZES

Dec 1 st at each end of next row. Work 3 rows.

Rep last 4 rows 0(1) time more.

Dec 1 st at each end of next and every foll alt row until 36(28:24:24)sts rem, ending with r.s. facing.

Dec 1 st at each end of every row until 24 sts rem.

Cast off rem sts.

MAKE UP, BANDS AND POCKET TOPS

Press lightly on w.s. with warm iron and damp cloth.

Join shoulders, using back stitch, adjust fullness at front to fit.

Join side and sleeve seams. Inset sleeves.

Button Band

With 3¼mm needles, cast on 9 sts.

1st row (R.S.), K2, * P1, K1: rep from * to last st, K1.

2nd row K1, * P1, K1; rep from * to end.

Rep these 2 rows until strip, when slightly stretched, fits up Right Front and round to centre back of neck. Sew in position as you go along. Cast off evenly in rib.

Buttonhole Band

Work as for Button Band with the addition of 7 buttonholes, first to come 1cm [½in] above lower edge, last to come level with start of front slope shaping and remainder spaced evenly between.

First mark positions of buttons with pins on Button Band to ensure even spacing, then work buttonholes to correspond.

To make a buttonhole: (R.S.), rib 3, cast off 2, rib to end and back casting on 2 over those cast off.

Join ends of Bands at back of neck.

Pocket Tops

With r.s. facing, 3¼mm needles, K across 36 sts of pocket dec 3 sts evenly. [33sts]

Work 9 rows in P1, K1, rib, rows on w.s. having a P1 at each end.

Cast off evenly in rib.

Catch down sides of Pocket Tops lightly to r.s. and Pocket Linings lightly on w.s.

Press seams.

Sew on buttons.

7 LUXURY FIBRES

Most luxury fibres are available from craft shops and are not at all difficult to handle and surprisingly inexpensive to use.

They are available in the form of combed tops which have been mechanically processed and are purchased as a continuous strand of parallel fibres, rather like a thick rope. These fibres should be pulled off at convenient lengths and then split into narrower strands for feeding onto the wheel. **They should NEVER BE CUT.**

If any of the yarns are obtained in woollen form, it is advisable to introduce more air into the fibres, thus making them go further, by lightly carding before spinning.

Whilst the following garments are made from using pure Llama, Alpaca, Cashmere, etc., it is possible and for more hard-wearing purposes practical to blend with wool on a two-thirds wool to one-third luxury yarn basis.

Annabel

Breed: Rabbit

This short-sleeved sweater has been knitted in pure angora wool, although it will look equally delightful knitted in any other yarn such as Romney or Shetland.

It has slightly puffed sleeves and the diamond panels have been enhanced with a small pearl bead in the centre.

MATERIALS

Hand Spun – Angora
9 threads per cm – Single ply
22 threads per in – Single ply

Commercial Equivalent – Double Knitting (thick)
5 threads per cm
12 threads per in

225(250:275:300)g of Angora.
Pair each 3mm and 4mm knitting needles.
Approx 380(400:420:440) small pearl beads.
NB If using a commercial yarn allow extra.

MEASUREMENTS

To fit bust 81(86:91:97)cm [32(34:36:38)in].
Length from top of shoulders 49(50:51:52)cm [$19\frac{1}{4}$($19\frac{3}{4}$:20:$20\frac{1}{2}$)in].
Sleeve seam 9cm [$3\frac{1}{2}$in].

TENSION

23 sts and 30 rows to 10cm [4in] measured over stocking stitch on 4mm needles.

94

27 Annabel

BACK

**With 3mm needles, cast on 94(100:106:112)sts and work in K1, P1 rib for 6cm [2¼in], inc 1 st at end of last row. [95(101:107:113)sts].

Change to 4mm needles and work in patt as folls:

1st row (R.S.), K31(34:37:40), [K2tog, yfwd, K1, yfwd, sl1, K1, psso, K2] 5 times, K29(32:35:38).

2nd row P30(33:36:39), [P2togtbl, yrn, P3, yrn, P2tog] 5 times, P30(33:36:39).

3rd row K31(34:37:40), [yfwd, sl1, K1, psso, K1, K2tog, yfwd, K2] 5 times, K29(32:35:38).

4th row P32(35:38:41), [yrn, P3tog, yrn, P4] 5 times, P28(31:34:37).

These 4 rows form patt.

Work straight in patt until Back measures 30cm [11¾in], ending with r.s. facing.

Shape armholes, keeping patt correct, by casting off 3(4:5:6)sts at beg of next 2 rows.

Dec 1 st at each end of next 3 rows, then dec 1 st at each end of every alt row until 73(75:79:83)sts rem.**

Work straight until armhole measures 19(20:21: 22)cm [7½(7¾:8¼:8¾)in], ending with r.s. facing.

Shape shoulders by casting off 6(6:7:7)sts at beg of next 4 rows, then 7(7:7:8)sts at beg of foll 2 rows.

Leave rem 35(37:37:39)sts on a spare needle.

FRONT

Work as for Back from ** to **.

Work straight until armhole measures 12(13:14: 15)cm [4¾(5:5½:6)in], ending with r.s. facing.

Divide for neck, keeping patt correct as folls:

Next row Patt 27(27:29:30), K2tog, turn and leave rem sts on a spare needle.

Dec 1 st at neck edge on every row until 19(19:21: 22)sts rem.

Work straight until Front matches Back to shoulder, ending with r.s. facing.

Shape shoulder by casting off 6(6:7:7)sts at beg of next and foll alt row.

Work 1 row, cast off rem 7(7:7:8)sts.

With r.s. facing, slip centre 15(17:17:19)sts on a length of yarn, rejoin yarn to rem sts, K2tog, patt to end.

Work to match first side, reversing shapings.

SLEEVES

With 3mm needles, cast on 56(56:58:58)sts and work in K1, P1 rib for 2cm [¾in].

Next row Rib 6(6:2:2), M1, [rib 2, M1] 22(22:27: 27) times, rib to end. [79(79:86:86)sts].

Change to 4mm needles and work in patt as folls:

1st row K2, * K2tog, yfwd, K1, yfwd, sl1, K1, psso, K2; rep from * to end.

2nd row P1, * P2togtbl, yrn, P3, yrn, P2tog; rep from * to last st, P1.

3rd row K2, * yfwd, sl1, K1, psso, K1, K2tog, yfwd, K2; rep from * to end.

4th row P3, * yrn, P3tog, yrn, P4; rep from * to last 6 sts, yrn, P3tog, yrn, P3.

These 4 rows form patt.

Work straight in patt until sleeves measures 9cm [3½in], ending with r.s. facing.

Shape top, keeping patt correct, by casting off 3(4:5:6)sts at beg of next 2 rows.

Dec 1 st at each end of next and every foll alt row until 45(33:38:36)sts rem, ending with r.s. facing.

Dec 1 st at each end of every row until 21(21:22: 22)sts rem.

Cast off rem sts.

MAKE UP AND NECK BORDER

Press lightly.

Join right shoulder.

Neck Border

With r.s. facing, 3mm needles, *Knit up* 19 sts down left side of neck, K15(17:17:19)sts from front, *Knit up* 19 sts up right side of neck, K35(37:37: 39)sts from back. [88(92:92:96)sts].

Work in K1, P1 rib for 5cm [2in].

Using a 4mm needle, cast off loosely in rib.

Join left shoulder and Neck Border.

Fold Neck Border in half to w.s. and slip hem loosely in position.

Join side and sleeve seams.

Insert sleeves.

Press seams.

Sew a bead to the centre of each diamond on Front and Sleeves.

Alexandra

Breed: Alpaca

An unusual effect has been created in this garment by using a combination of Fair Isle and lace. The main body of lace has a diamond pattern which has been echoed in the Fair Isle design on the yoke and sleeves.

ALPACA

Black/brown as the main shade in the lace pattern. Also used together with light brown and cream in the Fair Isle.

MATERIALS

Hand Spun – Alpaca
9 threads per cm – Single ply
22 threads per in – Single ply

Commercial Equivalent – Double Knitting (thick)
5 threads per cm
12 threads per in

325(350:375:400)g of Main Shade.
225(250:275:300)g of 1st Contrast.
60(75:90:105)g of 2nd Contrast.
Pair each 3¼mm, 4mm and 4¼mm knitting needles.
NB If using a commercial yarn allow extra.

MEASUREMENTS

To fit bust 81(86:91:97)cm [32(34:36:38)in].
Length from top of shoulders approx 56(57:58:59)cm [22(22½:22¾:23¼)in].
Sleeve seam 44cm]17¼in].

TENSION

19 sts and 28 rows to 10cm [4in] measured over lace pattern on 4mm needles.
22 sts and 23 rows to 10cm [4in] measured over Fair Isle on 4½mm needles.

Diagram 1 Chart for pattern of Alexandra

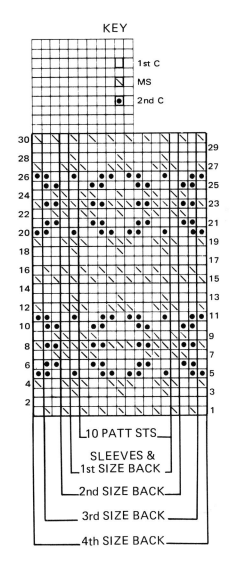

Note

When working from charts, strand yarn not in use loosely across w.s. of work over not more than 3sts at a time to keep fabric elastic.
Read odd rows K from right to left and even rows P from left to right.

SPECIAL ABBREVIATIONS

MS = Main Shade; 1st C = 1st Contrast; 2nd C = 2nd Contrast.

BACK

**With 3¼mm needles and MS, cast on 76(80:86: 90)sts and work in K1, P1 rib for 7cm [2¾in], inc 1 st at end of last row. [77(81:87:91)sts].

Change to 4mm needles and work in lace patt as folls:

1st row K6(3:6:3), * K2tog, yfwd, K1, yfwd, sl1, K1, psso, K5; rep from * to last 11(8:11:8)sts, K2tog, yfwd, K1, yfwd, sl1, K1, psso, K6(3:6:3).

2nd and every alt row P.

3rd row K5(2:5:2), * K2tog, yfwd, K3, yfwd, sl1, K1, psso, K3; rep from * to last 12(9:12:9)sts, K2tog, yfwd, K3, yfwd, sl1, K1, psso, K5(2:5:2).

5th row K4(1:4:1), * K2tog, yfwd, K5, yfwd, sl1, K1, psso, K1; rep from * to last 3(0:3:0)sts, K3(0:3:0).

7th row K5(2:5:2), * yfwd, sl1, K1, psso, K3, K2tog, yfwd, K3; rep from * to last 12(9:12:9)sts, yfwd, sl1, K1, psso, K3, K2tog, yfwd, K5(2:5:2).

9th row K6(3:6:3), * yfwd, sl1, K1, psso, K1, K2tog, yfwd, K5; rep from * to last 11(8:11:8)sts, yfwd, sl1, K1, psso, K1, K2tog, yfwd, K6(3:6:3).

11th row K7(4:7:4), * yfwd, sl2togk, K1, p2sso, yfwd, K7; rep from * to last 10(7:10:7)sts, yfwd, sl2togK, K1, p2sso, yfwd, K7(4:7:4).

12th row P.

These 12 rows form patt.

Work straight until Back measures approx 38cm [15in], ending with 10th(8th:4th::2nd) row of patt.

Shape armholes, keeping patt correct, by casting off 4(4:5:5)sts at beg of next 2 rows. Dec 1 st at each end of next and every foll alt row until 61(63:67:69)sts rem.

Work a few rows straight until armholes measures 5(6:7:8)cm [2(2¼:2¾:3¼)in], ending with 11th row of patt.

Next row P3(4:2:3), M1, [P6(6:7:7), M1] 9 times, P4(5:2:3). [71(73:77:79)sts].**

Change to 4½mm needles and joining in and breaking off colours as required work from chart, rep the 10 patt sts 7 times across and working end sts as indicated, until 30 rows of

28 Alexandra

chart have been completed.

Using 1st C, *shape shoulders* by casting off 7 sts at beg of next 4 rows, then cast off 6(6:7:7)sts at beg of foll 2 rows.

Leave rem 31(33:35:37)sts on a spare needle.

FRONT

Work as for Back from ** to **.

Change to 4½mm needles and joining in and breaking off colours as required, work from chart, rep the 10 patt sts 7 times across and working end sts as indicated, until 14 rows of chart have been completed.

Divide for neck, keeping patt correct, as folls:

Next row Patt 28(28:29:29)sts, K2tog, turn and leave rem sts on a spare needle.

Cont on these sts for first side, dec 1 st at neck edge on every row until 20(20:21:21)sts rem.

Work a few rows straight until Front matches Back to shoulder, ending with r.s. facing.

Using 1st C, *shape shoulder* by casting off 7 sts at beg of next and foll alt row.

Work 1 row. Cast off rem 6(6:7:7)sts.

With r.s. facing, slip centre 11(13:15:17)sts on a length of yarn, rejoin yarn to rem sts, K2tog, patt to end.

Work to match first side, reversing shapings.

SLEEVES

With 3¼mm needles and MS, cast on 42(44:44:46)sts and work in K1, P1 rib for 6cm [2¼in].

Next row Rib 1(4:4:5), M1, [rib 5(6:6:9), M1] 8(6:6:4) times, rib 1(4:4:5). [51sts].

Change to 4½ mm needles and joining in and breaking off colours as required, work from chart, rep the 10 patt sts 5 times across and working end sts as indicated for 1st Size on Back at the same time *shaping sides* by inc 1 st at each end of 5th and every foll 8th(7th:6th:6th) row until there are 69(73:75:77)sts, taking inc sts into patt.

Work straight until sleeve seam measures approx 44cm [17¼in], ending with 30th(28th:26th:24th) row of chart.

Shape top, keeping patt correct, by casting off 4(4:5:5)sts at beg of next 2 rows. Dec 1 st at each end of next and every foll alt row until 45(49:45:45)sts rem, ending with r.s. facing.

Dec 1 st at each end of every row until 21 sts rem. Cast off.

MAKE UP AND NECK BORDER

Press on wrong side of work, using a damp cloth and hot iron.

Join right shoulder seam.

Neck Border

With r.s. facing, 3¼mm needles and 1st C, *Knit up* 18 sts down left side of neck, K11(13:15:17)sts from front, *Knit up* 18 sts up right side of neck, K31(33:35:37)sts from back. [78(82:86:90)sts]. Break 1st C.

Using MS, P 1 row.

Work in K1, P1 rib for 2.5cm [1in].

Cast off loosely in rib.

Join left shoulder and Neck Border.

Join side and sleeve seams.

Insert sleeves.

Press seams.

Crystal

Breed: Goat

Pure luxury at its best, this pure cashmere sweater has a delightful cloverleaf eyelet pattern all over enhanced by a stocking stitch yoke, which has been trimmed with a knitted frill attached with velvet ribbon. As a final touch of class, tiny seed pearls have been sewn on at random.

MATERIALS

Hand Spun – Cashmere
9 threads per cm – Single ply
22 threads per in – Single ply

Commercial Equivalent – Double Knitting (thick)
5 threads per cm
12 threads per in

275(300:325:350)g of Cashmere.
Pair each 3mm and 4mm knitting needles.
90(100:110:120) small beads.
1 metre of velvet ribbon.
NB If using a commercial yarn allow extra.

MEASUREMENTS

To fit bust 81(86:91:97)cm [32(34:36:38)in].
Length from top of shoulders 56(57:58:59)cm [22(22½:22¾:23¼)in].
Sleeve seam 43cm [17in].

TENSION

24 sts and 32 rows to 10cm [4in] measured over stocking stitch on 4mm needles.

FRONT

**With 3mm needles, cast on 92(98:104:110)sts and work in K1, P1 rib for 7cm [2¾in].
Next row Rib 7, M1, [rib 13(14:15:16), M1] 6 times, rib 7. [99(105:111:117)sts].
Change to 4mm needles and work in patt as folls:
1st row K2(1:4:3), * yfwd, sl1, K2tog, psso, yfwd, K5; rep from * to last 1(0:3:2)sts, K1(0:3:2).
2nd and every alt row P.
3rd row K3(2:5:4), * yfwd, sl1, K1, psso, K6; rep from * to last 8(7:10:9)sts, yfwd, sl1, K1, psso, K6(5:8:7).
5th row K6(5:8:7), * yfwd, sl1, K2tog, psso, yfwd, K5; rep from * to last 5(4:7:6)sts, yfwd, sl1, K2tog, psso, yfwd, K2(1:4:3).
7th row K8(7:10:9), * yfwd, sl1, K1, psso, K6; rep from * to last 4(3:6:5)sts, yfwd, sl1, K1, psso, K2(1:4:3).
8th row P.
These 8 rows form patt.**
Work straight until Front measures approx 35cm [13¾in], ending with 4th or 8th row of patt.
Commence yoke as folls:
Next row Patt 47(50:53:56), K2tog, yfwd, K1, yfwd, K2togtbl, patt 46(49:52:55).
Next row P.
Next row Patt 46(49:52:55), K2tog, yfwd, K3, yfwd, K2togtbl, patt 46(49:52:55).
Next row P.
Cont thus, working 1 st less in patt on each side, taking them into centre panel as before *at the same time* shape armholes by casting off 3(3:4:4)sts at beg of next 2 rows.
Dec 1 st at each end of next 3 rows. Work 1 row.
Dec 1 st at each end of next and every foll alt row until 75(79:83:85)sts rem.
Cont working straight until the row 'patt 15, K2tog, yfwd, K41(45:49:51), yfwd, K2togtbl, patt 15' has been worked.
Work 1 row.
Divide for front neck as folls:
Next row Patt 14, K2tog, yfwd, K11(13:14:15), K2tog, turn and leave rem sts on a spare needle.
Cont on these sts for first side, dec 1 st at neck edge on every row until 20(21:22:22)sts rem.
Work a few rows straight until the row 'patt 4, K2tog, yfwd, K14(15:16:16)' has been worked. Work 1 row.
Shape shoulder by casting off 7 sts at beg of next and foll alt row.
Work 1 row. Cast off rem 6(7:8:8)sts.
With right side facing, slip centre 17(17:19:19)sts on a spare needle, rejoin yarn to rem sts, K2tog, patt to end.
Work to match first side, reversing shapings.

29 Crystal

BACK

Work as for Front from ** to **.

Work straight in patt until Back matches Front to armholes, ending with same row of patt.

Shape armholes, keeping patt correct, by casting off 3(3:4:4)sts at beg of next 2 rows, then dec 1 st at each end of foll 3 rows. Work 1 row.

Dec 1 st at each end of next and every foll alt row until 75(79:83:85)sts rem.

Work straight in patt until Back matches Front to shoulder, ending with r.s. facing.

Shape shoulders by casting off 7 sts at beg of next 4 rows, then 6(7:8:8)sts at beg of foll 2 rows.

Leave rem 35(37:39:41)sts on a spare needle.

SLEEVES

With 3mm needles, cast on 52(54:56:58)sts and work in K1, P1 rib for 6cm [2¼in].

Next row Rib 5(5:3:5), M1, [rib 7(11:5:6), M1] 6(4:10:8) times, rib 5(5:3:5). [59(59:67:67)sts].

Change to 4mm needles and work in patt as given for 1st Size on Front, *shaping sides* by inc 1 st at each end of 9th and every foll 12th(8th:12th:8th) row until there are 75(83:83:91)sts, taking inc sts into patt.

Work straight until sleeve measures 43cm [17in], ending with same row of patt as on Front and Back.

Shape top, keeping patt correct, by casting off 3(3:4:4)sts at beg of next 2 rows.

Dec 1 st at each end of next and every foll alt row until 29(41:33:37)sts rem, ending with r.s. facing.

2ND, 3RD AND 4TH SIZES

Dec 1 st at each end of every row until 29 sts rem.

ALL SIZES

Cast off 2 sts at beg of next 2 rows.

Cast off rem 25 sts.

MAKE UP AND NECK BORDER

Join right shoulder seam.

Neck Border

With r.s. facing, 3mm needles, *Knit up* 18 sts down left side of neck, K17(17:19:19)sts from front, *Knit up* 18 sts up right side of neck, K35(37:39:41)sts from back. [88(90:94:96)sts].

Work in K1, P1 rib for 5cm [2in].

Using a 4mm needle, cast off loosely in rib.

Join left shoulder and Neck Border.

Fold Neck Border in half to w.s. and slip-hem loosely in position.

Join side and sleeve seams.

Insert sleeves.

Frill

With 4mm needles, cast on 331(351:371:391)sts and work as folls:

1st row P2, * K7, P3; rep from * to last 9 sts, K7, P2.

2nd row K2, * P7, K3; rep from * to last 9 sts, P7, K2.

3rd row P2, * K2togtbl, K3, K2tog, P3; rep from * to last 9 sts, K2togtbl, K3, K2tog, P2.

4th row K2, * P5, K3; rep from * to last 7 sts, P5, K2.

5th row P2, * K2togtbl, K1, K2tog, P3; rep from * to last 7 sts, K2togtbl, K1, K2tog, P2.

6th row K2, * P3, K3; rep from * to last 5 sts, P3, K2.

7th row P2, * sl1, K2tog, psso, P3; rep from * to last 5 sts, sl1, K2tog, psso, P2.

8th row K2, * P1, K3; rep from * to last 3 sts, P1, K2.

9th row P1, [K2tog, yfwd] 32(34:36:38) times, P1, K1, P1, [yfwd, K2tog] 32(34:36:38) times, P1.

10th row K1, P to last st, K1.

Cast off.

Thread ribbon through frill and holes on yoke, secure on w.s.

Attach frill at shoulders.

Press seams.

Stitch beads at random over garment.

Lynnet

Breed: Llama

An elegant double-breasted jacket in pure Llama for a luxurious garment, completed with hand-carved horn buttons.

MATERIALS

Hand Spun – Llama
8 threads per cm – Single ply
20 threads per in – Single ply

Commercial Equivalent – Aran type (thin)
4.5 threads per cm
11 threads per in

800(850:875:900:975)g of Llama.
Pair each 4mm and 4½mm knitting needles.
8 Buttons.
NB If using a commercial yarn allow extra.

MEASUREMENTS

To fit bust 81(86:91:97:102)cm [32(34:36:38:40)in].
Length from top of shoulders 62(63:64:65:67)cm [24½(24¾:25¼:25½:26½)in].
Sleeve seam 43cm [17in].

TENSION

18 sts and 24 rows to 10cm [4in] measured over stocking stitch on 4½mm needles.
24 sts and 30 rows to 10cm [4in] measured over K1, P1 rib on 4mm needles.

BACK

With 4mm needles, cast on 77(81:87:91:97)sts and work in K1, P1 rib for 3cm [1¼in], rows on r.s. having a K1 at each end, ending with r.s. facing.
Change to 4½mm needles and starting with a K row, work in st.st. until Back measures 42cm [16½in], ending with a P row.

Shape armholes by casting off 4(4:5:5:6)sts at beg of next 2 rows, then dec 1 st at each end of every alt row until 57(59:61:65:67)sts rem.
Work straight until Back measures 62(63:64:65:67)cm, ending with r.s. facing.
Shape shoulders by casting off 5(6:6:6:6)sts at beg of next 4 rows, then 6(5:5:6:6)sts at beg of foll 2 rows.
Leave rem 25(25:27:29:31)sts on a spare needle.

POCKET LININGS (2)

With 4½mm needles, cast on 18 sts and starting with a K row, work in st.st. for 6cm [2¼in], ending with a P row. Leave sts on a spare needle.

LEFT FRONT

**With 4mm needles, cast on 25(27:29:31:33)sts and work in K1, P1 rib as given for Back, inc 1(1:1:0:0)st at end of last row. [26(28:30:31:33)sts].
Change to 4½mm needles and starting with a K row, work in st.st. until Front measures 9cm [3½in], ending with a P row.**
Place Pocket as folls:
Next row K5(7:9:10:12), slip next 18 sts on a length of yarn and in place of these K across 18 sts of first pocket lining, K to end.
Work straight until Front matches Back to armhole less 2 rows.
Place False Pocket as folls:
Next row K10(12:14:15:17), slip next 13 sts on a spare needle, turn and cast on 13 sts, turn, K to end. Work 1 row.
Shape armhole by casting off 4(4:5:5:6)sts at beg of next row. Work 1 row.
Dec 1 st at armhole edge on next and every alt row until 16(17:17:18:18)sts rem.
Work straight until Front measures 55(56:57:58:60)cm [21¾(22:22½:22¾:23½)in], ending with a P row.
Place a marker at beg of last row on front edge.
Work straight until Front matches Back to shoulder, ending with r.s. facing.
Shape shoulder by casting off 5(6:6:6:6)sts at beg of next and foll alt row.
Work 1 row. Cast off rem 6(5:5:6:6)sts.

30 Lynnet

RIGHT FRONT

Work as for Left Front from ** to **.

Place pocket as folls:

Next row K3, slip next 18 sts on a length of yarn and in place of these K across 18 sts of second pocket lining, K to end.

Work as for Left Front, reversing shapings and omitting false breast pocket.

SLEEVES

With 4mm needles, cast on 40(42:42:44:44)sts and work in K1, P1 rib for 3cm [1¼in].

Change to 4½mm needles and starting with a K row, work in st.st. *shaping sides* by inc 1 st at each end of 3rd and every foll 8th(8th:7th:7th:7th) row until there are 60(64:66:68:70)sts.

Work straight until sleeve measures 43cm [17in], ending with r.s. facing.

Shape top by casting off 4(4:5:5:6)sts at beg of next 2 rows.

4TH AND 5TH SIZES

Dec 1 st at each end of next row. Work 3 rows.

Rep last 4 rows 0(2) times more.

ALL SIZES

Dec 1 st at each end of next and every alt row until 18(22:18:18:18)sts rem, ending with r.s. facing.

2ND SIZE

Dec 1 st at each end of every row until 18 sts rem.

ALL SIZES

Cast off rem sts.

MAKE UP COLLAR AND BORDERS

Press lightly on w.s. with a damp cloth and warm iron.

Join shoulder seams.

Left Front Border

With 4mm needles, cast on 33(35:37:39:41)sts and work as folls:

1st row (R.S.), K2, * P1, K1,; rep from * to last st, K1.

2nd row K1, * P1, K1; rep from * to end.

Rep these 2 rows until Border fits up Left Front to marker, ending with r.s. facing. Sewing in posi-

tion as you go along. Cast off neatly in rib.

Right Front Border

Work as for Left Front Border with the addition of 4 sets of 2 buttonholes. Mark position of buttons on Left Front, first set to come 2cm [¾in] from lower edge of Jacket and last level with start of armhole shaping, the others spaced evenly between.

Buttonhole Row

(R.S.), Rib 4, cast off 3 sts, rib to last 8 sts, cast off 3, rib to end, and back again casting on 3 sts over those cast off.

Collar

With r.s. facing, starting at marker on Right Front, with 4mm needles, *Knit up* 22 sts to shoulder, K25(25:27:29:31)sts from back, *Knit up* 22 sts to marker on Left Front. [69(69:71:73:75)sts].

Next row P4(4:3:4:4), M1, [P2, M1] 31(31:33:33:35) times, P3(3:2:3:2). [101(101:105:107:111)sts].

Work in rib as given for Left Front Border until Collar measures 8(8:8:9:9)cm [3¼(3¼:3¼:3½:3½)in].

Cast off neatly in rib.

False Pocket Top

With r.s. facing, 4mm needles, K across 13 sts left at armhole, inc 2 sts evenly. [15sts].

Work in P1, K1 rib for 2cm [¾in], rows on w.s. having a P1 at each end, ending with r.s. facing.

Cast off evenly in rib.

Pocket Tops

With r.s. facing, 4mm needles, K across 18 sts on a length of yarn, inc 3 sts evenly. [21sts].

Work in P1, K1 rib for 3cm [1¼in], rows on w.s. having a P1 at each end, ending with r.s. facing.

Cast off evenly in rib.

Catch down sides of Pocket Tops neatly to r.s. of work and Pocket Linings lightly on w.s.

Join side edges of Collar to Front Borders to form revers.

Join side and sleeve seams.

Insert sleeves.

Press seams.

Sew on Buttons.

8 FUN FIBRES

Most dogs when shedding their winter coats in the spring emit at first a very fine 'down' undercoat that is very soft and suitable for spinning. It seems a pity not to use these combings.

We are nowadays used to seeing garments made from the hair of Samoyed, Pyrenean Mountain and perhaps German Shepherd or Collie but even the Yellow Labrador gives off a soft peach undercoat and blended with short lambswool will give a lovely hank of yarn just itching to be knitted!

If we bear in mind 'If it keeps them warm, it will keep us warm' and start collecting there will be a totally free source of lovely fibres just waiting to be used.

Samantha

Category: Shortwool and Down
Breed: Shetland
Other Fibres: Samoyed dog hair

A unique use of dog hair featured as the contrast in this round-yoked sweater gives this garment a touch of difference! Complete with pretty matching hat.

MATERIALS

Hand Spun – Shetland
8 threads per cm – Single ply
20 threads per in – Single ply

Hand Spun – Samoyed
As for Shetland.

Commercial Equivalent – Aran type (thin)
4.5 threads per cm
11 threads per in

Sweater
450(475:525:550)g of Shetland.
25(25:30:30)g of Samoyed.

Hat
50g of Shetland.
5g of Samoyed.
Pair each 3¾mm and 4½mm knitting needles.
A set of four 3¾mm and 5mm double pointed needles or circular 3¾mm and 5mm needles.
NB If using a commercial yarn allow extra.

MEASUREMENTS

Sweater
To fit bust 81(86:91:97)cm [32(34:36:38)in].
Length from top of shoulders 60(61:62:63)cm [23½(24:24½:24¾)in].
Sleeve seam 46cm [18in].

Hat
To fit average head.

31 Samantha

TENSION

18 sts and 24 rows to 10cm measured over stocking stitch on 4½mm needles.

SPECIAL ABBREVIATIONS

MS = Main Shade; C = Contrast.

Sweater

BACK

**With 3¾mm needles and MS, cast on 72(78:82: 88)sts and work in K1, P1 rib for 6cm [2¼in].
Next row Rib 4(4:6:5), M1, [rib 9(10:10:11), M1] 7 times, rib to end. [80(86:90:96)sts].
Change to 4½mm needles and work in st.st. until Back measures 38cm [15in], ending with a P row.**
Shape armholes by casting off 4(4:5:5)sts at beg of next 2 rows.

1ST, 3RD AND 4TH SIZES
Dec 1 st at each end of next row. Work 3 rows.
Rep last 4 rows 0(2:2) times more.

1ST, 2ND AND 4TH SIZES
Dec 1 st at each end of next row. Work 1 row.
Rep last 2 rows 0(3:0) times more.

ALL SIZES
Leave rem 68(70:74:78)sts on a spare needle.

Note
When working from charts, strand yarn not in use loosely across w.s. of work over not more than 3 sts at a time to keep fabric elastic.
For Chart A, read rounds from right to left working all rounds in K.
For Chart B, read odd rows K from right to left and even rows P from left to right.

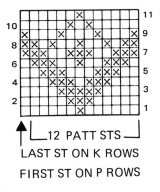

KEY

☐	MS
☒	C
	K2 tog
	K2 tog tbl

CHART A

12 PATT STS

CHART B

12 PATT STS
LAST ST ON K ROWS
FIRST ST ON P ROWS

Diagram 2 Charts for pattern of Samantha

FRONT

Work as for Back from ** to **.
Shape armholes and *divide for neck* as folls:

1ST SIZE

1st row Cast off 4 sts, K21 [including st on needle after cast off], turn and leave rem sts on a spare needle.
2nd and every alt row Sl1, P to end.
3rd row K2tog, K13, turn.
5th row K8, turn.
7th row K2tog, K2, turn.
8th row Sl1, P to end.
Slip 19 sts of side neck onto a length of yarn.

2ND, 3RD AND 4TH SIZES

Cast off 4(5:5)sts at beg of next 2 rows.

3RD AND 4TH SIZES

Dec 1 st at each end of next row. Work 3 rows.

4TH SIZE

Dec 1 st at each end of next row. Work 1 row.

2ND, 3RD AND 4TH SIZES

Divide for neck as folls:

1st row K2(2:0)tog, K22(22:26), turn and leave rem sts on a spare needle.
2nd and every alt row Sl1, P to end.
3rd row K2(0:2)tog, K15(17:18), turn.
5th row K2(2:0)tog, K8(9:11), turn.
7th row K2(0:2)tog, K3(4:4), turn.
8th row Sl1, P to end.
Slip 20(22:24)sts of side neck on a length of yarn.

ALL SIZES

With r.s. facing, slip centre 30 sts on a length of yarn, rejoin yarn to rem sts and complete to match first side, reversing shapings.

SLEEVES

With 3¾mm needles and MS, cast on 40(42:42:44)sts and work in K1, P1 rib for 6cm [2¼in].
Next row Rib 5(6:6:5), M1, [rib 10(10:10:11), M1] 3 times, rib to end. [44(46:46:48)sts].
Change to 4½mm needles and work in st.st. *shaping sides* by inc 1 st at each end of 3rd and every foll 8th row until there are 64(66:68:70)sts.
Work straight until sleeve measures 46cm [18in], ending with a P row.

Shape armholes by casting off 4(4:5:5)sts at beg of next 2 rows.

1ST, 3RD AND 4TH SIZES

Dec 1 st at each end of next row. Work 3 rows.
Rep last 4 rows 0(2:2) times more.

1ST, 2ND AND 4TH SIZES

Dec 1 st at each end of next row. Work 1 row.
Rep last 2 rows 0(3:0) times more.

ALL SIZES

Leave rem 52(50:52:54)sts on a spare needle.

YOKE AND NECK BORDER

With r.s. facing slip 34(35:37:39)sts of Back onto a spare needle
Using either circular or set of four 5mm needles, K34(35:37:39)sts from back, 52(50:52:54)sts from sleeve, 68(70:74:78)sts from front, 52(50:52:54)sts from sleeve, 34(35:37:39)sts from back. Mark beg of rounds. [240(240:252:264)sts].
Joining in C, work 38 rounds from chart A, rep the 12 patt sts 20(20:21:22) times and dec where indicated. [80(80:84:88)sts].
Break C and work 1 round in MS.
Next round [K8, K2tog] 10 times, K0(0:4:8). [72(72:76:80)sts].
Change to 3¾mm circular needle and work in rounds of K1, P1 rib for 7cm [2¾in].
Using a 5mm needle, cast off loosely in rib.

MAKE UP

Join armholes, side and sleeve seams.
Fold Neck Border in half to w.s. and slip-hem loosely in position.
Press seams.

HAT

With 3¾mm needles and MS, cast on 97 sts and work in K1, P1 rib for 3cm [1¼in].
Change to 4½mm needles and work 2 rows in st.st.
Change to 5mm needles and joining in C as required, work 11 rows from chart B, rep the 12 patt sts 8 times across and working last st on K rows and first st on P rows as indicated.
Change to 4½mm needles and work straight in st.st.

until Hat measures 15cm [6in], ending with r.s. facing.

Shape crown as folls:

1st row *K6, K2tog; rep from * to last st, K1. [85sts].

2nd and every alt row P.

3rd row *K5, K2tog; rep from * to last st, K1. [73sts].

5th row *K4, K2tog; rep from * to last st, K1. [61sts].

Cont thus dec until 25 sts rem, ending with a P row.

Next row K3tog, * K2tog; rep from * to end. [12sts].

Break yarn, thread through rem sts, draw up tightly and fasten off securely.

Join back seam.

Make a pompom with MS and attach to top of hat.

Press seam.

9 CREATING A PORTFOLIO

A very useful portfolio can be compiled that will be of help to all knitters. One suggestion is to record notes as shown in the following example.

1 *Category:* Shortwool and Down
2 *Fleece:* Shetland
3 *Handspun threads:* 10 per cm   25 per in
4 *Dye section:*
(a) Commercial Kit or ready prepared dyes
Quantities used:
Samples of colour:

(b) Natural dyes
Quantities of fibres or materials used:
Samples of colour:

(c) Blend
Combinations used:
Samples of colours attained:

5 *Tension:* 24 sts and 36 rows over pattern.
6 *Knitted sample square:*
(Attach here a knitted sample c. 10×10cm (4 × 4 in) of the garment.)
7 *Needles used:* 4mm

8 *Design:* Round neck, long sleeves, lacey pattern with ribbed shoulders

9 *Quantity of yarn used:* 250g for a 86cm [34 in]

10 *Commercial equivalent:* Double knitting (thin)

11 *Commercial threads:* 5.5 per cm   14 per in

12 *Any other information:*

That beautiful yarn created by mistake, when recorded, can be an instant recall for all time!

10 TECHNICAL INFORMATION

TENSION

Correct tension is essential.

To Check Your Tension

Cast on the given number of stitches for 10cm [4in] and work the number of rows as stated, either in stocking stitch or pattern, whichever is quoted on the design you wish to knit.

If the square is bigger than 10cm [4in], your work is too loose; try a size finer needle.

If the square is smaller, your work is too tight; try a size larger needle. Any alteration in needle size should be continued throughout the design.

NB A difference of 1cm [$\frac{1}{2}$in] on your tension square means an additional 9cm [$3\frac{1}{2}$in] on a garment size of 86cm [34in], therefore the extra time spent working on a tension square means the difference between a garment that fits perfectly and one that does not.

KNITTING NEEDLES (sizes)

Metric (in mm)	Britain	USA
2	14	00
2¼	13	0
2¾	12	1
3	11	2
3¼	10	3
3½ and 3¾	9	4
4	8	5
4½	7	6
5	6	7
5½	5	8
6	4	9
6½	3	10
7	2	10½
7½	1	11
8	0	—
8½	00	13
9	000	15

GRAM TO OUNCE CONVERSION

gram	ounce	gram	ounce
25	1	275	$9\frac{3}{4}$
50	$1\frac{3}{4}$	300	$10\frac{1}{2}$
75	$2\frac{3}{4}$	325	$11\frac{1}{2}$
100	$3\frac{1}{2}$	350	$12\frac{1}{4}$
125	$4\frac{1}{2}$	375	$13\frac{1}{4}$
150	$5\frac{1}{4}$	400	14
175	$6\frac{1}{4}$	425	15
200	7	450	$15\frac{3}{4}$
225	8	475	$16\frac{3}{4}$
250	$8\frac{3}{4}$	500	$17\frac{3}{4}$

*The above conversions are approximate. 1 ounce = 28.35 grams approximately.

METRIC TO IMPERIAL CONVERSION

cm	in	cm	in
1	$\frac{1}{2}$	26	$10\frac{1}{4}$
2	$\frac{3}{4}$	27	$10\frac{3}{4}$
3	$1\frac{1}{4}$	28	11
4	$1\frac{1}{2}$	29	$11\frac{1}{2}$
5	2	30	$11\frac{3}{4}$
6	$2\frac{1}{4}$	31	$12\frac{1}{4}$
7	$2\frac{3}{4}$	32	$12\frac{1}{2}$
8	$3\frac{1}{4}$	33	13
9	$3\frac{1}{2}$	34	$13\frac{1}{2}$
10	4	35	$13\frac{3}{4}$
11	$4\frac{1}{4}$	36	$14\frac{1}{4}$
12	$4\frac{3}{4}$	37	$14\frac{1}{2}$
13	5	38	15
14	$5\frac{1}{2}$	39	$15\frac{1}{4}$
15	6	40	$15\frac{3}{4}$
16	$6\frac{1}{4}$	41	16
17	$6\frac{3}{4}$	42	$16\frac{1}{2}$
18	7	43	17
19	$7\frac{1}{2}$	44	$17\frac{1}{4}$
20	$7\frac{3}{4}$	45	$17\frac{3}{4}$
21	$8\frac{1}{4}$	46	18
22	$8\frac{3}{4}$	47	$18\frac{1}{2}$
23	9	48	19
24	$9\frac{1}{2}$	49	$19\frac{1}{4}$
25	$9\frac{3}{4}$	50	$19\frac{3}{4}$

* The above conversions are approximate.

1 in = 2.54cm

Abbreviations

and American equivalents for British terms

alt = alternate (USA: every other)

approx = approximately

beg = beginning

cast off = USA: bind off

ch = chain

cm = centimetre

dc = double crochet (USA: single crochet)

foll = following

g = gram

in = inch

inc = increase

K = Knit

M1 = make one stitch by picking up horizontal loop lying before next stitch and working into back of it

mm = millimetre

P = Purl

patt = pattern

psso = pass slip stitch over

rep = repeat

shape top = USA: shape cap

sl = slip

sl1 K = slip 1 Knitways

sl1 P = slip 1 Purlways

st.st. = stocking stitch

st(s) = stitch(es)

tbl = through back of loops

tension = USA: gauge

tog = together

yb = yarn back

yft = yarn front

yfwd = yarn forward

yrn = yarn round needle

yon = yarn on needle

g.st. = garter stitch

r.s. = right side

w.s. = wrong side

sl2togK = slip 2 sts together as if to K2tog

p2sso = pass 2 slip sts over

List of suppliers

GREAT BRITAIN

General

Bodeilio Weaving & Craft
  Centre
Talwrn, Nr. Llangefni
Anglesey
Gwyndd

Campden Weavers
16 Lower High St
Chipping Campden
Glos GL55 6DY

Craft Technique
19 Old Orchard St
Bath, Avon

Dryad
P.O. Box 38
Northgates
Yorks

Handweaver's Studio &
  Gallery
29 Haroldstone Road
London E17 7AN

Helios Fountain
7 Grassmarket
Edinburgh

Kineton Gallery
Banbury St
Kineton
Warwickshire CV35 0JS

Little London Spinners
7 Tee Court
Bell St
Romsey
Hants SO5 8GY

Elizabeth Palmer
Crown Cottage
46 High St
Gretton
Corby
Northants

Ruth Palfrey
South Hill Farm
Yeoford
Crediton
Devon

Shuttlewood Studio
Friars Walk, Friars Lane
Maldon
Essex CM9 6AG

Spinners
Eileen Ringwood
Brickyln Farm, Hoe
Dereham
Norfolk NR19 2CR

Susan Foster
9 Windermere Road
Kendal
Cumbria

Textile Workshop & Gallery
166 High St
Edinburgh

Wingham Wool Work
The Building Yard
Rotherham Road
Wentworth
S. Yorks

Fleeces

British Wool Marketing Board
Kew Bridge House
Brentford
Middlesex TW8 0EL

Cotswold Farm Park
Bemborough
Guiting Power, Glos

Jacob Fleece Society
Sec. Mrs John Thornley
St Leonards
Tring, Herts

Local Wool Staplers
Craftsman's Mark Ltd
  (Wool Matchings)
Trefnant
Denbigh, Clwyd

Hair fibres

Cottage Crafts
1 Aked Street
Bradford

Dyes & Mordants

London Textile Workshop
65 Roseberry Road
London N10 2LE

Matheson Dyes & Chemicals
Marcon Place
London E8 1LP

Seeds

John & Caroline Stevens
Sawyers Farm, Little Cornard
Sudbury
Suffolk

Other Useful Addresses

British Wool Marketing Board
Oak Mills
Clayton
Bradford
West Yorks BD14 6JD

Rare Breeds Survival Trust
4th St
N.A.C. Stoneleigh Park
Kenilworth
Warks CV8 2LG

Association of Guilds of Weavers,
  Spinners and Dyers
c/o Five Bays
10 Stancliffe Avenue
Marford, Wrexham, Clwyd

CoSIRA
141 Castle Street
Salisbury
Wiltshire

Crafts Council
12 Waterloo Place
London SW1Y 4AU

Federation of British Craft Societies
British Craft Centre
43 Earlham St
London WC2

London Guild of Weavers, Spinners and Dyers
c/o 80 Scotts Lane
Bromley
Kent

USA
International Handspinning Directory
Mrs Kenneth Chapin
2178 Pompey-Fabius Road
RD 1 Fabius
New York

Shuttle, Spindle and Dyepot
1013 Farmington Avenue
West Hertford
Conn 06107

Handweavers' Guild of America Inc
65 La Salle Road
West Hartford
Conn 06107

The following magazines give information on equipment and materials:

The Weaver's Journal
The Colorado Fiber Center
P.O. Box 2049
Boulder
Colorado 80306

Fiberarts
50 College St
Asheville
North Carolina 28801

Interweave
2938 North Country Road
Loveland
Colorado 80537

AUSTRALIA
Crafts Council of A.C.T.
Canberra Spinners and Weavers
Crafts Council of New South Wales
Handweavers and Spinners Guild of Australia
Crafts Council of Queensland
Queensland Spinners Weavers and Dyers Group
Crafts Council of South Australia
Handweavers and Spinners Guild of S.A.
Crafts Council of Tasmania
Handweavers Spinners and Dyers Guild of
  Tasmania
Crafts Council of Victoria
Handweavers and Spinners Guild of Victoria
Crafts Council of Western Australia
Handweavers and Spinners Guild of W.A.
Crafts Council of Australia, Sydney

Bibliography

Adrosko, Rita. *Natural Dyes and Home Dyeing.* New York, 1971.

Bliss, Anne. *A Handbook of Dyes from Natural Materials.* New York, 1983.

Brown, Rachel. *The Weaving, Spinning, and Dyeing Book.* New York, 1978.

Castino, Ruth, and Marjorie Pickens. *Spinning and Dyeing the Natural Way.* New York, 1974.

Davenport, Elsie. *Your Handspinning.* London, 1953.

Goodwin, Jill. *A Dyer's Manual.* London, 1982.

Howar, V. *Weaving, Spinning, and Dyeing: A Beginner's Manual.* Englewood Cliffs, NJ, 1976.

Jackson, Constance, and Judith Plowman, *The Woolcraft Book: Spinning, Dyeing, and Weaving.* New York, 1983.

Kiewe, H. E. *The Sacred History of Knitting.* Oxford, 1967.

Ross, Mabel. *The Essentials of Handspinning.* Spinning Dale, Crook of Devon, Kinross, Scotland, 1980.

Ross, Mabel. *The Essentials of Yarn Design for Handspinners.* Spinning Dale, Crook of Devon, Kinross, Scotland, 1983.

Ryder, Michael. *Sheep and Wool for Handicraft Workers.* Edinburgh, 1978.

Thomas, Mary. *Mary Thomas's Book of Knitting Patterns.* New York, 1972.

Index

abbreviations 115
alpaca 97
  garments made from:
    Alexandra – Fair Isle and lace patterned sweater 97
American sheep breeds 13, 14
angora 38, 94
animal fibres 107

beads 48, 94, 101
blending 38, 39, 42, 61, 72, 94, 107
Bradford count 13, 14
breeds 13
British Wool Marketing Board 13
buttons 32, 48, 104

carding 38, 61, 72, 94
cashmere 38, 101
  garments made from:
    Crystal – sweater 101
cat 38
chart 12, 97, 109
Cheviot 21, 90
  garments made from:
    Cheryl – waistcoat 21
    Craig – man's V-neck cardigan 90
commercial dyed yarns 61, 90
  garments made from:
    Dulcie – diamond patterned sweater 62
    Ivy – bomber jacket 78
    Joseph – child's jumper 65
    Louise – stocking stitch sweater 75
    Morwenna – dropped shoulder sweater 81
    Penelope – lace and moss stitch sweater 84
    Rosetta – waistcoat 72
    Sarah – girl's jumper 68
commercial dyes, use of 87, 90
  garments made from:
    Craig – man's V-neck cardigan 90
    Petula – knitted coat 87

dog hair 38, 75, 107
  garments made from:
    Samantha – round yoke sweater and hat 107

fun fibres 107
  garments made from:
    Samantha – round yoke sweater and hat 107

glitter yarn (commercial) 45, 51
goat 38, 72, 81, 101

Herdwick yarn 32, 90
  garments made from:
    Heath – man's jacket 32

Jacob sheep 14, 38, 87
  garments made from:
    Jamesina – slash neck sweater 14
    Joanna – stole 24
    Petula – knitted coat 87

lambswool 72, 84, 87
  garments made from:
    Penelope – lace and moss stitch sweater 84
    Petula – coat 87
    Rosetta – waistcoat 72
llama 104
  garments made from:
    Lynnet – double-breasted jacket 104
Longwool and Lustre 13, 65, 68, 81
luxury fibres 94, 97, 101, 104

measuring of yarns 11
micron system 13
mohair 38, 39, 42, 72, 87
  garments made from:
    Louise – stocking stitch sweater 75
    Michael – V-neck cabled sweater 42
    Morag – V-neck sweater 39
    Morwenna – dropped shoulder sweater 81
    Petula – knitted coat 87
    Rosetta – waistcoat 72

natural dyeing 61, 90
needles 113

plying 14, 45, 56
pure wool 13

rabbit 94
  garments made from:
    Annabel – short sleeved sweater 94
ribbons 17, 21, 26, 29, 53, 60, 72, 84
Romney 13, 65, 68, 94
  garments made from:
    Joseph – child's jumper 65
    Morwenna – dropped shoulder sweater 81
    Sarah – girl's jumper 68
Ross System 11

Shetland sheep 14, 45, 94
    garments made from:
        Dorothea – lace patterned sweater 35
        Elizabeth – smocked cardigan 48
        Guinevere – wedding dress 17
        Helen – triangular shawl – 51
        Isobel – frilled V-neck sweater 53
        Kirsty – lace yoked sweater 27
        Lavinia – lace panelled sweater 29
        Louise – stocking stitch sweater 75
        Michael – V-neck cabled sweater 42
        Morag – V-neck sweater 39
        Petula – knitted coat 87
        Samantha – round yoke sweater 107
        Thane – lace and cabled patterned sweater 45
Shortwool and Down 13, 17, 25, 29, 35, 39, 42, 48,
      51, 53, 84, 87, 94
silk 45, 48, 51, 53, 56, 72, 75, 84
    bombyx 45
    garments made from:
        Caroline – camisole 56

        Elizabeth – smocked cardigan 48
        Helen – triangular shawl 51
        Isobel – frilled V-neck sweater 53
        Louise – stocking stitch sweater 75
        Penelope – lace and moss stitch sweater 94
        Rosetta – waistcoat 72
        Sabrina – skirt and jacket 56, 57
        Thane – lace and cabled pattern sweater 45
    tussah 56
    waste 56
smocking 48
S-twist 11

technical information 113
tensions 113
tops 62, 65
T-twist directions 11

unplyed yarns 24

Z-twist 11